HOW TO BE CARING

ANCIENT WISDOM FOR MODERN READERS

■ ■ ■ ■

HOW TO BE CARING

ANCIENT WISDOM FOR MODERN READERS

■ ■ ■ ■

HOW TO BE CARING

■ ■ ■ ■ ■

An Ancient Guide to a Compassionate Life

Shantideva

Selected, translated, and introduced by
Jay L. Garfield

PRINCETON UNIVERSITY PRESS
PRINCETON AND OXFORD

Published by Princeton University Press
41 William Street, Princeton, New Jersey 08540
99 Banbury Road, Oxford OX2 6JX

press.princeton.edu

GPSR Authorized Representative: Easy Access System
Europe - Mustamäe tee 50, 10621 Tallinn, Estonia,
gpsr.requests@easproject.com

All Rights Reserved

ISBN 9780691274072
ISBN (e-book) 9780691274065

Library of Congress Control Number: 2025930825

British Library Cataloging-in-Publication Data is available

Editorial: Rob Tempio and Chloe Coy
Production Editorial: Mark Bellis
Text and Jacket Design: Heather Hansen
Production: Erin Suydam
Publicity: William Pagdatoon and Charlotte Coyne
Copyeditor: Plaegian Alexander

Jacket Credit: Lhasa gTsug lag khang; inventory no. 602[A]
from *Buddhist Sculptures in Tibet, Vol. Two: Tibetan & Chinese*,
pp. 1078–1079, pl. 279C. von Schroeder, Ulrich. 2001.
Photo by Ulrich von Schroeder (1996).

This book has been composed in Stempel Garamond with Futura

Printed and bound by CPI Group (UK) Ltd, Croydon, CR0 4YY

1 3 5 7 9 10 8 6 4 2

For Blaine, whose friendship, care, joy in the happiness of others, and concern for everyone has sustained me all these years

CONTENTS

CONTENTS

INTRODUCTION

We don't know much about Shantideva (Śāntideva). We do know that the author of *How to
Lead an Awakened Life* (*Bodhicāryāvatāra*)—the
text from which these verses are drawn—lived in
the eighth century and taught at Nalanda University, which was in the present-day state of Bihar
in eastern India. From its founding in the fifth
century until its destruction in the late twelfth
century, it was the largest, most cosmopolitan
university in the world, and its ruins, even though
only partly excavated, are dramatic.

Regarding Shantideva, we have only legend.
Here is the story of his life that we find in Buddhist
canonical literature: Shantideva had a reputation
for being very lazy. His colleagues said of him

that all he did was eat, sleep, and shit. So one day, in order to embarrass him publicly, they invited him to give a talk in the main lecture hall to a huge assembly of students and scholars. He asked them whether they wanted him to talk about something old or to present some new ideas. They asked for the latter.

On the appointed day, Shantideva settled on the high teaching throne and recited the poetic text of *How to Lead an Awakened Life*. Upon concluding the lecture (and wowing the audience with what was to become one of the most beloved texts of the Mahayana—the Great Vehicle—tradition), he rose into the air and flew from the lecture hall, disappearing into space, never to be seen again. When some of his fellow monks went to his room, they found two books: *How to Lead an Awakened Life* and its companion reader, *A Student's Anthology* (*Śikṣasamuccaya*).

We know a bit more about *How to Lead an Awakened Life* itself than we do about its initial author. In particular, we know that it was edited and reedited over the first century or so of its existence, with two principal versions in circulation under slightly different titles. The older version is shorter (about 700 verses); the longer version (about 900 verses, of which we present 150 here) not only includes many verses not included in the shorter version but also rearranges the earlier text, moving many verses from one chapter to another. There are also some discrepancies between the latest Sanskrit version we have and the Tibetan edition, which seems to be drawn from a still later edition. Some people like to think of the oldest version as the *authentic* text and the later ones as distortions; I prefer to think of the older versions (and we really don't know whether we have the *oldest*) as rough drafts and the latest version as the final draft. In any case, it is a fairly late version that is the subject of Indian commentaries, and Tibetan commentaries follow the Tibetan edition from which the verses in this volume are drawn.

How to Lead an Awakened Life is one of the most beloved and frequently taught texts in the Indo-Tibetan Mahayana tradition. It is a favorite of the present Dalai Lama, and he often teaches it in public. It is the most systematic presentation of ethical thought in that tradition and is composed in beautiful poetry that appeals to scholars and to laypeople alike. The topic of the text is the life of a bodhisattva (a person committed to attaining awakening for the benefit of all beings) represented as a path of ethical cultivation leading to awakening.

The bodhisattva's commitment, called *bodhicitta* (the resolve to awaken), is the hallmark of the Mahayana practitioner. In a religious context, such a person resolves to attain the status of a buddha—to become omniscient and supremely skillful—and, instead of leaving existence in order to enter into nirvana, to remain in order to help others become liberated from the suffering of life. This resolve is motivated by the attitude of *care* (*karuṇā*), which is one of the four "divine moral attributes" in Buddhist moral theory. (The others are friendliness, impartiality, and the ability to rejoice in the success of others.) Care in this sense is the commitment to relieve suffering.

But all this does not mean that this text is only of use to serious Buddhist practitioners. It speaks to all of us. We can understand this aspiration in a more modern, secular vein as the resolve to become the most effective agents possible for the betterment of the world and for the relief of suffering. Shantideva's core insight is that because there is so much suffering in the world, and because its alleviation is often so difficult, if we are to become effective, caring

agents for the improvement of life, we must assiduously cultivate ourselves as moral agents—
that is, the first step to solving the problems of
the world is to conquer our own psychopathologies and to become better, more caring people.
And that insight speaks to us just as it did to
medieval Buddhist monks in India. This book is
about how to become that kind of moral agent.

In selecting the verses from *How to Lead and
Awakened Life* to present here, I have focused
on those that have a universal audience—that
do not rely on specifically ancient Indian Buddhist doctrines. By doing so, I am able to present the specifically ethical line of argument in
a way that should make sense to all readers, regardless of their religious commitments or lack
thereof. This does mean, however, that there are
issues of importance to Śāntideva himself and
to those who read him in a specifically Buddhist

context that are not represented here, such as the cosmology of rebirth, the nature of karma, and some of the scholastic internecine debates that arise in chapter 9. Those who are interested in these issues and their bearing on the ethical advice presented here are encouraged to read the entire text.

The book is oriented on four axes, and part of its elegance lies in the fact that it advances simultaneously on each of them. First, it follows the stages of the path of the bodhisattva as set out in the sutra *Discourse on the Ten Grounds* and in the *Bodhisatva Stages* by Asanga, a fourth-century scholar. In these and other related texts, the bodhisattva's progress to awakening is set out in stages, with particular moral qualities perfected at each stage. The qualities Shantideva addresses and the order in which he discusses them follow that framework.

Second, Shantideva adopts a distinction drawn by Chandrakirti (Candrakīrti), his seventh-century Nalanda predecessor, between different ways we may consider beings as objects of our care. The first aspect is sentient beings appearing *as sufferers*. We apprehend others, see their suffering, and resolve to alleviate it. This is the most basic way to see others as needing our care. This way of seeing others motivates us to help, but it gives us neither a deep understanding of that suffering nor a clear sense of how to alleviate it.

The second aspect is sentient beings appearing *as dependently originated*. When we see sentient beings this way, we apprehend them with the realization that their situations, their actions, and their suffering are caused by countless causes and conditions outside of their control, and that the appearance of autonomy is always an illusion. To see them this way allows us to step back from attitudes of praise and blame toward others, and to replace anger toward sources of harm with patience. It is also to replace pride in our own accomplishments and shame for our failures with gratitude and self-understanding. It is to focus more on the web of conditions that enable or trap us than on ourselves or others as independent individuals. Seeing beings this way allows us to intervene skillfully in order to alleviate the conditions that cause suffering and to provide the conditions for greater happiness.

Chandrakirti and Shantideva think that the most sensitive way to apprehend sentient beings, though, is through a third aspect as *empty of any fixed nature* and thus constantly changing and always appearing to one another in an illusory way—appearing to have fixed and immutable natures when instead they are constantly in flux. When we see ourselves and others this way, we shed our preconceptions; we don't impose our sense of who others must be on them or act in ways that reflect a preconception of who we are; we engage in a more spontaneous, perceptual, expert way. This is like the difference between beginners and expert musicians, athletes, or cooks: Beginners think things through, but their performance is rather clunky; experts achieve grace by transcending explicit thought.

When we consider these three aspects under which we may experience ourselves and others, we see a kind of progress from clueless desire to help to the commitment to understanding how to help, culminating in a spontaneous skill in helping to remove suffering. Think for instance of what may lead someone to take up medicine and what their career may look like. Asha, a college sophomore, goes to a remote village in a jungle to do some anthropological fieldwork.

While there, she realizes that the people she is studying suffer from a range of debilitating and painful diseases. *Seeing their suffering*, she decides to forgo the study of anthropology and to take up the study of medicine.

After completing medical school, first as an intern and then as a resident, Asha comes to understand better how the body works, how diseases arise, and how cures work. Seeing the *dependence* of people's suffering, she comes to see her patients as complex systems of organs interacting with the environment and with pathogens; she develops her clinical skills, studying each patient with care and consulting carefully before prescribing a course of treatment. Her patients and colleagues respect her skill but find her a bit cold and, one may say, *clinical*.

After a few years of practice, though, Asha no longer sees complex systems in her examining

INTRODUCTION

room; she sees people *in constant flux*; she reacts to them with warmth and care, without *projecting a theory of who they are or what is wrong with them*, and that spontaneous vision of who they are leads to a more spontaneous sense of what they need. Her old skills do not vanish, but they now serve a more humane interaction with her patients. This is the doctor she trained to become. Shantideva asks us to train to become mature, expert moral agents, motivated by others' suffering and by our own and informed by our understanding of interdependence but seeing and acting with effortless spontaneity.

The third axis is one that Shantideva introduces in verses 15 and 16 of chapter 1—that is, the transition from an aspirational to an engaged resolve to awaken. The first attitude reflects a conceptual understanding of suffering and of the nature of human existence as well as a philosophical commitment to the view that it would be good for one to become a more perfect agent for the relief of suffering through cultivating one's moral and intellectual skills. This is a fine attitude to motivate one to improve oneself, but it falls short of the attitude that underlies the kind of expertise and character one hopes to develop. Engaged resolve, in contrast, is grounded not in theoretical understanding but in direct perceptual and affective engagement with the world and with others.

To engage is to *see* suffering, not just to know about it; to engage is to *feel* the need to alleviate suffering, not just to know that alleviating it would be a good thing. This book is also about how to make the transition from the aspirational resolve that Shantideva compares to the discursive knowledge of a distant place, which one may glean from a guidebook or from Tripadvisor, to the engaged resolve that he compares to the perceptual knowledge that one achieves from traveling to that place. The one who has read the guidebook may know a lot about the place, but it is the one who has traveled there who *really* knows what the place is like. The one who has cultivated aspirational resolve has a reason to become a better person; the one who has cultivated engaged resolve has truly become a better person.

The final axis on which this text is oriented is a ritual axis. The entire text is structured on the pattern of a classic nine-part Indian Buddhist offering ritual. We need not worry about the details here. The important point is that Shantideva (and his subsequent editors) saw this poem not merely as a book *about* ethics, not merely as *advice,* but as transformative prayer—that is, Shantideva envisioned his reader as joining him in the project of self-transformation through the ritual of reading. For this reason, the text is written in a gripping, first-person, confessional voice, sometimes expressing remorse, sometimes resolve, and often resolution. Shantideva writes explicitly to himself, urging himself to become a better, more rational, more caring agent; but when he addresses himself, he is addressing the reader as well, inviting you into his inner moral world and into the project of self-cultivation on which he is embarked.

The text thus has an urgency to it. Shantideva invites you to read with him in the first person and to experience this text in your own voice. Even when the text shifts from first- to second-person voice, the second person is Shantideva addressing himself, or it is you, the reader, addressing yourself. It is never one person addressing another but instead a kind of self-exhortation.

This personal voice, as much as the deep insight the text conveys, is responsible for the text's enormous power and popularity. I invite you to read this text in the spirit in which Shantideva offers it, as an experience of self-transformation.

Thanks to Douglas Duckworth, Jonathan Gold, Maria Heim, Emily McRae, and Andy Rotman for helpful comments on previous drafts.

HOW TO BE CARING

1. FIRST, KEEP THIS IN MIND: YOU WILL NOT LIVE FOREVER!

Shantideva begins by reminding himself—and inviting us to remind ourselves—of the urgency of the moral task at hand. This task is that of transforming ourselves from ordinary agents of suffering into agents for the relief of suffering, or replacing our egocentric orientation to the world with a caring orientation to everyone. This is no mean feat. And, Shantideva asks us to remind ourselves, our lives are limited. We are urged to remember that we now have the opportunity to undertake this transformative journey. We don't know how long our lives will be or what misfortunes we may encounter later that may make it difficult to make real moral progress. So there is no time to lose!

The verses drawn from the beginning of chapter 1 emphasize the value of the opportunity we have—life, good health, and time to devote ourselves to contemplation and self-improvement. Verses 1.15 and 1.16 introduce us to the difference between merely thinking about becoming agents of change and actually doing so. And the verses drawn from chapter 2 bring us face-to-face with our own imminent demise. This may seem morbid, but Shantideva wants to remind us that to fail to think about our own death is to fail to recognize the most important aspect of our life; to keep death in the forefront of our consciousness is not only realistic and healthy but also the best motivation for seizing the time we have.

In a classical Indian context, such as that in which Shantideva lived, many people would think of this motivation in terms of karma and rebirth. *Karma* literally means "action," yet can also mean "the effects of action." So, to talk about karma is to talk about action and its effects. Taken literally, belief in rebirth is the belief that after death, another being psychologically connected to us will be born and will experience the effects of actions we have performed. Those who take this view seriously will want to make sure that while alive, they perform effects that will have positive results for their successors.

But we don't have to think this way to take karma and the future seriously. The actions we perform now all have effects after our deaths. How we travel and heat our houses will affect the lives of those who come after us; whether we work for peace or make war will have effects after our death; how we raise our children will also have such effects. So, we don't have to think about the future in terms of *personal* rebirth in order to care about it. These verses urge us to take our mortality seriously because we only have so much time to make sure that our lives are not harmful but beneficial to those who come after us, and they urge us to take seriously the long-term consequences of whatever we do.

1.4

དལ་འབྱོར་འདི་ནི་རྙེད་པར་ཤིན་ཏུ་དཀའ།།
སྐྱེས་བུའི་དོན་སྒྲུབ་ཐོབ་པར་གྱུར་པ་ལ།།
གལ་ཏེ་འདི་ལ་ཕན་པ་མ་བསྒྲུབས་ན།།
ཕྱིས་འདི་ཡང་དག་འབྱོར་པ་ག་ལ་འགྱུར།། ༩

1.5

ཇི་ལྟར་མཚན་མོ་མུན་ནག་སྤྲིན་རུམ་ན།།
གློག་འགྱུ་སྐད་ཅིག་རབ་སྣང་སྟོན་པ་ལྟར།།
དེ་བཞིན་སངས་རྒྱས་མཐུ་ཡིས་བརྒྱ་ལམ་ན།།
འཇིག་རྟེན་བསོད་ནམས་བློ་གྲོས་ཐང་འགའ་འབྱུང་།། ༥

1.6

དེ་ལྟས་དགེ་བ་ཉམ་ཆུང་ཉིད་ལ་རྟག།།
སྡིག་པ་སྟོབས་ཆེན་ཤིན་ཏུ་མི་བཟད་པ།།
དེ་ནི་རྫོགས་པའི་བྱང་ཆུབ་སེམས་མིན་པ།།
དགེ་གཞན་གང་གིས་ཟིལ་གྱིས་གནོན་པར་འགྱུར།། ༧

. . . . .

1.4

It is so hard to find the time and tools I need
To help those with whom I share this world.
If I don't seize the chance now,
It may never arise again!

1.5

Just as a thunderbolt
Can light a dark cloudy night for an instant,
An awakened being can sometimes
Inspire people to do the right thing.

1.6

Virtue is so feeble;
Vice is so powerful and terrible!
How can good ever triumph over evil
Without the resolve to awaken?

. . . . .

1.8

སྲིད་པའི་ཕྱུག་བསྐལ་བརྒྱ་ཕྲག་གཞོམ་འདོད་ཅིང་།།
སེམས་ཅན་མི་བདེ་བསལ་བར་འདོད་པ་དང་།།
བདེ་མང་བརྒྱ་ཕྲག་སྤྱོད་པར་འདོད་པས་ཀྱང་།།
བྱང་ཆུབ་སེམས་ཉིད་རྟག་ཏུ་གཏང་མི་བྱ།།

1.15

བྱང་ཆུབ་སེམས་དེ་མདོར་བསྡུས་ན།།
རྣམ་པ་གཉིས་སུ་ཤེས་བྱ་སྟེ།།
བྱང་ཆུབ་སྨོན་པའི་སེམས་དང་ནི།།
བྱང་ཆུབ་འཇུག་པ་ཉིད་ཡིན་ནོ།།

1.16

འགྲོ་བར་འདོད་དང་འགྲོ་བ་ཡི།།
བྱེ་བྲག་ཇི་ལྟར་ཤེས་པ་ལྟར།།
དེ་བཞིན་མཁས་པས་འདི་གཉིས་ཀྱི།།
བྱེ་བྲག་རིམ་བཞིན་ཤེས་པར་བྱ།།

. . . . .

1.8

If I want to vanquish the suffering of the world,
Relieve the suffering of all beings,
And find true joy in life
I must never abandon the resolve to awaken!

1.15

In brief, there are two kinds
Of resolve to awaken:
Aspirational resolve
And engaged resolve.

1.16

Just as you can tell the difference between
One who is planning a trip and one who has been
    there,
A smart person can tell
The difference between these two kinds of resolve.

. . . . .

2.32

བདག་ནི་སྲིག་པ་མ་བྱུང་བར།།

སྟོན་དུ་འགྱུམ་པར་འགྱུར་དུ་མཆི།།

ཇི་ལྟར་འདི་ལས་ངེས་ཐར་བར།།

གྱུར་བའི་ཚུལ་གྱིས་བསླབ་དུ་གསོལ།།

2.33

ཡིད་བརྟན་མི་རུང་འཆི་བདག་འདི།།

བྱས་དང་མ་བྱས་མི་སྟོད་པས།།

ན་དང་མི་ན་ཀུན་གྱིས་ཀྱང་།།

གློ་བུར་ཆེ་ལ་ཡིད་མི་བརྟན།།

2.34

ཐམས་ཅད་བོར་ཏེ་ཆ་དགོས་པར།།

བདག་གིས་དེ་ལྟར་མ་ཤེས་པས།།

མཛའ་དང་མི་མཛའི་དོན་གྱི་ཕྱིར།།

སྲིག་པ་རྣམ་པ་སྣ་ཚོགས་བྱས།།

2.32

Death may overtake me
While I am still consumed by vice!
How can I escape this fate?
Somebody, please help me!

2.33

Death arrives like a bolt of lightning,
He doesn't care what I have done or left
    undone.
Neither the healthy nor the ailing
Should ever trust such an enemy!

2.34

I have done terrible things,
Both for friends and to enemies.
And I have never even thought,
"When I die, I will leave them all behind."

2.37

རེ་ཞིག་གསེར་ཆེ་འདི་ཉིད་ལ་འབད།།
མཐའ་དང་མི་མཐའ་དུ་མ་འདས།།
དེ་དག་དོན་དུ་བྱས་པའི་སྒྲིག
མི་བཟད་གང་ཡིན་མདུན་ན་གནས།། ༣༠

2.38

དེ་ལྟར་བདག་ནི་བློ་བུར་ཞེས།།
བདག་གིས་རྟོགས་པར་མགྱུར་པས།།
གཏི་མུག་ཆགས་དང་ཞེ་སྡང་གིས།།
སྒྲིག་པ་རྣམ་པ་དུ་མ་བྱས།། ༣༠

2.41

གཞན་རྗེའི་ཕོ་ཉས་རིན་པ་ལ།།
གཉེན་གྱིས་ཅི་ཕན་བཤེས་ཅི་ཕན།།
དེ་ཚེ་བསོད་ནམས་གཅིག་སྐྱབས་ན།།
དེ་ཡང་བདག་གིས་མ་བསྟེན་ཏོ།། ༧༡

1 2

2.37
In my own lifetime, I have seen
friends and enemies pass away.
But the misdeeds I have done for their sake
Remain behind and continue to fester.

2.38
Still, I have not noticed
That I, too, am ephemeral.
Because of attraction, aversion, and confusion,
I have done many terrible things.

2.41
Of what use are friends and family
When I am in the arms of the minions of death?
Only my virtue can help me then,
And so far, I haven't cultivated it!

2.58

དེ་རིང་ཁོ་ན་མི་འཆི་ཞེས།།
བདེ་བར་འདུག་པ་རིགས་མ་ཡིན།།
བདག་ནི་མེད་པར་འགྱུར་བའི་དུས།།
དེ་ནི་གདོན་མི་ཟ་བར་འབྱུང་།།

༥༨

2.61

གསོན་ཚེ་འདད་དང་དེ་བཞིན་དུ།།
གཉེན་དང་བཤེས་པ་རྣམས་སྤངས་ནས།།
གཅིག་པུ་ག་ཤེད་འགྲོ་དགོས་ན།།
མཛའ་དང་མི་མཛའ་ཀུན་ཅི་རུང་།།

༧༡

2.62

མི་དགེ་བ་ལས་སྡུག་བསྔལ་འབྱུང་།།
དེ་ལས་ཇི་ལྟར་ངེས་ཐར་ཞེས།།
ཉིན་མཚན་རྟག་ཏུ་བདག་གིས་ནི།།
འདི་ཉིད་འབའ་ཞིག་བསམ་པའི་རིགས།།

༧༢

2.58
So it makes no sense for me to relax and say,
"I won't die today."
It is certain that the time will come
When I will no longer exist.

2.61
I will say goodbye to kith and kin,
And to the land of the living.
Since I will depart alone.
What good are friends and foes to me
    even now?

2.62
The only thing that it makes sense to ask,
Day and night, is this:
How can I avoid the suffering
Caused by a vicious life?

2. NEXT, THINK ABOUT WHAT IS MOST IMPORTANT!

In this next set of verses, drawn principally from the chapter on vigilance, Shantideva asks us to focus on what is most important in our lives. It is easy to become complacent, to think that a good life is a life of pleasure and to feel that our happiness is threatened by adversities that befall us from outside.

Shantideva urges us to reconsider. Instead, he argues, a good life is a life in which we contribute to collective well-being, and true happiness lies not in our own pleasure but in the satisfaction that such contribution brings. But most importantly, he argues that we misidentify the threats to our happiness when we look outside. Instead, our own everyday psychopathologies—our self-absorption, our tendencies to be attracted to trivial things and annoyed by unimportant irritations, and our misperceptions of reality—are the real causes of unhappiness.

So, he tells us, if we want to be happy, we need to direct our efforts at self-improvement, not to acquiring more things or to eliminating the external annoyances in our everyday lives. Only then can we have any hope of being truly happy and of becoming the kind of person who can bring happiness to others.

The way to do that, Shantideva argues, is not just to develop the *wish* to become a better person but to take a *vow* to do so, or as we may put it, to adopt a *resolution.* This is not a promise that we make to others; instead, it is a firm commitment that becomes part of our own psychological attitude toward the world, framing all our other goals and intentions. And, given what we learned in the previous chapter, the time to begin that process of self-improvement is *now!*

4.23

འདི་འདྲའི་དལ་བ་རྙེད་གྱུར་ནས།།
བདག་གིས་དགེ་གོམས་མ་བྱས་ན།།
འདི་ལས་བསླུས་པ་གཞན་མེད་དེ།།
འདི་ལས་རྨོངས་པའང་གཞན་མེད་དོ།།

23

4.24

གལ་ཏེ་བདག་གིས་དེ་རྟོགས་ནས།།
རྨོངས་པས་ཕྱིས་ཀྱང་སྙིད་ལུག་ན།།
འཆི་བར་འགྱུར་བའི་དུས་ཀྱི་ཚེ།།
མྱ་ངན་ཆེན་པོ་ལྡང་བར་འགྱུར།།

24

. . . . .

4.28

ཞེ་སྡང་སྙེད་སོགས་དགྲ་རྣམས་ནི།།
རྐང་ལག་ལ་སོགས་ཡོད་མིན་ལ།།
དཔའ་མཛངས་མིན་ཡང་ཇི་ཞིག་ལྟར།།
དེ་དག་གིས་བདག་བྲན་བཞིན་བྱས།།

28

WHAT IS MOST IMPORTANT

4.23
Nothing could be more self-deceptive,
Or more delusional,
Than not acting virtuously
When I have the chance to do so.

4.24
If I already know this,
But, in the throes of delusion, still remain lazy,
Just think how terrible I will feel
When the moment of death arrives!

. . . . .

4.28
My real enemies are attraction and aversion.
They have no arms or legs;
They are neither brave nor clever.
So, how have they managed to enslave me?

4.29

དབག་གི་སེམས་ལ་གནས་བཞིན་དུ།།
དགའ་མགུར་བདག་ལ་གནོད་བྱེད་པ།།
དེ་ལའང་མི་གྲོ་བཟོད་པ་ནི།།
གནས་མིན་བཟོད་པ་སྐྱེད་པའི་གནས།།

༢༩

4.32

བདག་གི་ཉེན་མོངས་དགྲས་པོ་གང་།།
དུས་རིང་ཐོག་མཐའ་མེད་པ་ལྟར།།
དགྲ་ཞན་ཀུན་ཀྱང་དེ་ལྟ་བུར།།
ཡུན་རིང་ཐུབ་པ་མ་ཡིན་ནོ།།

༣༢

4.33

མཐུན་པར་རིམ་གྲོ་བསྟེན་བྱས་ན།།
ཐམས་ཅད་ཕན་དང་བདེ་བྱེད་ན།།
ཉོན་མོངས་རྣམས་ནི་བསྟེན་བྱས་ན།།
ཕྱིར་ཞིང་སྡུག་བསྔལ་གནོད་པ་བྱེད།།

༣༣

WHAT IS MOST IMPORTANT

4.29

I allow them to dwell in my own mind,
And I entertain them while they destroy me.
I even tolerate this shameful situation
Without the slightest embarrassment!

4.32

None of my other enemies
Live as long as my pathologies!
They have lived with me for so long
That they appear to be endless!

4.33

When I treat people well,
They are kind and helpful.
But when I treat these enemies well,
They just bring me endless suffering.

4.34

དེ་ལྟར་ཡུལ་རིང་རྒྱུན་ཆགས་དགར་གྱུར་པ།།
གཞོན་པའི་ཚོགས་རབ་འཕེལ་བའི་རྒྱུ་གཅིག་པུ།།
བདག་གི་སྙིང་ལ་ངེས་པར་གནས་འཆའ་ན།།
འཁོར་བར་འཇིགས་མེད་དགའ་བར་ག་ལ་འགྱུར།། ༣༨

4.36

དེ་ལྟར་དེ་སྲིད་བདག་གིས་དགའ་འདི་མཛེན་སུམ་དུ།།
ངས་པར་མ་བཅོམ་དེ་སྲིད་བདག་འདིར་བརྩོན་མི་འདོར།།
རེ་ཞིག་གཞོན་བྱེད་ཀྱང་དུ་ལ་ཡང་གྲོས་གྱུར་པ།།
ང་རྒྱལ་བདོ་རྣམས་དེ་མ་བཅོམ་པར་བཉིད་མི་འོང་།། ༣༧

4.39

དོན་མེད་དགྲ་ཡིས་རྨ་སྲོལ་བཏོད་པ་ཡང་།།
ལུས་ལ་རྒྱན་དང་འདྲ་བར་སྲེལ་བྱེད་ན།།
དོན་ཆེན་སྒྲུབ་ཕྱིར་ཡང་དག་བརྩོན་གྱུར་པ།།
བདག་ལ་སྡུག་བསྔལ་ཅི་ཕྱིར་གནོད་བྱེད་ཡིན།། ༣༠

22

WHAT IS MOST IMPORTANT

4.34

How can I enjoy life
When these eternal enemies
Are ensconced fearlessly in my heart,
Causing endless problems?

4.36

So, I will not give up my quest until
I see for myself that these foes are destroyed,
Just as those swollen with pride
Cannot rest until those who have insulted them
   are slain.

4.39

When soldiers pointlessly
Wear battle scars as jewelry,
Then, when I have a a great aim,
Why should I allow some suffering to deter me?

4.40

ཏུ་པ་གདོལ་པ་ཞིང་པ་ལ་སོགས་པ།།
རང་གི་འཚོ་བ་ཚམ་ཞིག་སེམས་པ་ཡད།།
གྱུང་དྲང་ཚལ་སོགས་པའི་གནོད་བཟོད་ན།།
འགྲོ་བ་བདེ་ཕྱིར་བདག་ལྟ་ཅིས་མི་བཟོད།།

༼༠

4.41

ཕྱོགས་བཅུ་ནམ་མཁའི་མཐའ་བདུགས་པའི།།
འདོ་བ་ཉེན་མོངས་ལས་བསྒྲལ་བར།།
དམ་བཅས་གང་ཚེ་བདག་ཉིད་ཀྱང་།།
ཉེན་མོངས་རྣམས་ལས་མ་གྲོལ་བར།།

༼༡

. . . . .

7.64

སྦུ་གྱིའི་སོར་ཆགས་སྒྱུང་ཅི་སྟེའི།།
འདོད་པ་རྣམས་ཀྱིས་མི་ངོམས་ན།།
ཁན་སྙིན་བདེ་ལ་ཞི་བ་ཡི།།
བདོད་ནམས་ཀྱིས་ལ་ཅི་སྟེ་ངོམས།།

༼༩

WHAT IS MOST IMPORTANT

4.40
And if fishermen, farmers, and servants,
Who only think of their own survival,
Patiently endure the pains of heat and cold,
Can't I be steadfast in this battle for the good
    of all beings?

4.41
But even though I have vowed to free
All beings wherever they are in the world,
I have not yet freed myself
From my own pathologies!

. . . . .

7.64
Pleasure is like honey on a razor's edge;
It leads to no real happiness.
How much better are the fruits of virtue
That ripen in joy and peace!

3. BE GENEROUS!

Shantideva now begins characterizing and recognizing the principal virtues or perfections to be cultivated on the path to awakening. The first of these is generosity. Generosity is usually understood in Buddhist literature in terms of three kinds of gifts and in terms of two levels of the virtue itself. The kinds of gifts are material goods, comfort or refuge from fear, and teachings or mentorship. Each of these is something that is in our power to offer others, and each is mentioned in some of the verses presented here.

Generosity can be either mundane or supramundane. Mundane generosity is generosity in which we consciously identify ourselves as givers, those to whom we give as beneficiaries, and that which we give as a gift. It is what we often do when we undertake what fundraisers call "planned giving." Supramundane generosity is a spontaneous activity in which we do not thematize these roles, in which we are simply generous without even thinking about it, as in a flow state. Shantideva envisions a progress from the mundane to the supramundane as part of moral cultivation—that is, our goal in this domain is for giving to be as natural as inhaling and exhaling. As the Indigo Girls sing, "Love is just like breathing when it's true," a state that they, like Shantideva, identify as a kind of freedom.

Generosity is obviously good for others—for those to whom one is generous. But here Shantideva emphasizes that generosity is also good for the generous person. The point is not just that generosity makes us better people in virtue of the fact that we are beneficial to others in the world — though of course it does. Generosity is also a source of happiness and satisfaction for the one who gives.

This is true in two important senses. First, every time we give, we reduce our attachment to our own goods. It is not just that giving gets easier with practice; it is that our innate attachment to our own possessions, our own time, or our own knowledge is reduced, and mundane giving gradually becomes supramundane. That reduction in attachment inevitably increases our happiness by reducing our need for possessions and our anxiety about losing them.

But giving, as Shantideva also recognizes, also allows us to see our lives as meaningful, and that means that generosity is also a great gift that we can bestow on ourselves. Returning to the importance of the mindfulness of death: On our deathbeds, we will not want think that our lives have been worth living simply because we accumulated possessions or got really smart; instead, we will want to think that our lives have been meaningful because of the help they were able to provide for others.

Finally, note that while Shantideva sees the goal of our cultivation of moral excellence to be an extraordinary level of generosity, he recognizes that reaching this level of moral expertise is hard and takes time. He therefore suggests that we start by handing out zucchini from our gardens. But our goal is to become as generous as firefighters who are willing to rush into a burning building, risking their lives and literally giving their own flesh to save others.

3.7

འགོ་བ་ནད་པ་རྗེ་སྐྱིད་ལྡ།།

ནད་སོས་གྱུར་གྱི་བར་དུ་ནི།།

སྨན་དང་སྨན་པ་ཉིད་དག་དང་།།

དེ་ཡི་ནད་གཡོག་བྱེད་པར་ཤོག།   ७

3.8

ཟས་དང་སྐོམ་གྱི་ཆར་ཕབ་སྟེ།།

བཀྲེས་དང་སྐོམ་པའི་གནོད་པ་བསལ།།

མུ་གེའི་བསྐལ་པ་བར་མའི་ཚེ།།

བདག་ནི་ཟས་དང་སྐོམ་དུ་གྱུར།།   ८

3.9

སེམས་ཅན་ཕོངས་ཤིང་དབུལ་བ་ལ།།

བདག་ནི་མི་ཟད་གཏེར་གྱུར་ཏེ།།

ཡོ་བྱད་མཁོ་དགུ་སྣ་ཚོགས་སུ།།

མདུན་ན་ཉེ་བར་གནས་གྱུར་ཅིག།   ९

30

BE GENEROUS

3.7

For as long as beings are ill,
Until they are all cured,
Let me be their doctor,
Their medicine, and their nurse.

3.8

Let me slake their hunger and thirst
By showering food and drink;
Let me *be* the very food and drink
For those beset by famine.

3.9

Let me be an endless treasury
For the destitute;
Let me stay with them
To help in any way that I can!

3.10

ལུས་དང་དེ་བཞིན་ལོངས་སྤྱོད་དང་༎
དུས་གསུམ་དགེ་བ་ཐམས་ཅད་ཀྱང་༎
སེམས་ཅན་ཀུན་གྱི་དོན་བསྒྲུབ་ཕྱིར༎
ཕངས་པ་མེད་པར་གཏང་བར་བྱ༎ ༡༠

3.11

ཐམས་ཅད་བཏང་བས་མྱ་ངན་འདའ༎
བདག་བློ་མྱ་ངན་འདས་པ་བསྒྲུབ༎
ཐམས་ཅད་གཏོང་བར་ཆབས་ཅིག་ལ༎
སེམས་ཅན་རྣམས་ལ་གཏང་བ་མཆོག༎ ༡༡

3.13

བདག་གི་ལུས་ལ་ཇི་བྱེད་དམ༎
ཅི་འདྲི་ག་ཞིའི་རྒྱུ་བྱེད་ཀྱང་༎
ཉེཨག་གི་ལུས་འདི་བྱིན་ཟིན་གྱིས༎
འདི་ཡི་ཁ་ཏས་ཅི་ཞིག་བྱ༎ ༡༣

32

BE GENEROUS

3.10

I will happily relinquish my body,
My pleasure, and even my own virtue
If that will help others
To achieve their goals.

3.11

To give up everything is to be free,
And freedom is my goal!
Since I give it all up anyway,
It is best to give it to others while I am still here.

3.13

Maybe they'll treat me like a plaything;
Maybe they'll make fun of me. So what?
Since I have already given myself to them,
Why should I care what they do with me?

3.14

དེ་ཨོལ་གནོད་པར་མི་འགྱུར་བའི།།

ལས་གང་ཡིན་པ་འང་བྱེད་དེ་རྒྱག།

བདག་ལ་དམིགས་ནས་ནམ་དུ་ཡང་།

འགའ་ཡང་དོན་མེད་མ་གྱུར་ཅིག །

༡༤

3.15

བདག་ལ་དམིགས་ནས་གང་དག་གིས།།

ཁྲོ་འམ་དད་པའི་སེམས་སུ་བྱུང་ན།།

དེ་ཉིད་རྟག་ཏུ་དེ་དག་གི །

དོན་ཀུན་འགྲུབ་པའི་རྒྱུར་གྱུར་ཅིག །

༡༥

3.16

གང་དག་བདག་ལ་ཁ་ཟེར་རམ།།

གཞན་དག་གནོད་པ་བྱེད་པ་འམ།།

དེ་བཞིན་ཕར་ཀ་གཏོང་ཡང་རུང་།

ཐམས་ཅད་བྱང་ཆུབ་སྐལ་ལྡན་གྱུར།།

༡༦

. . . . .

BE GENEROUS

3.14

As long as it causes them no harm,
I will do whatever they want.
If they come to me for help,
Let that not be in vain.

3.15

Whether they come to me
In anger or with respect,
Let them always succeed
In getting what they need.

3.16

May even those who cause me harm,
Disrespect and slander me,
And even those who disparage me
Achieve full awakening!

. . . . .

3.17

བདག་ནི་མགོན་མེད་རྣམས་ཀྱི་མགོན།།

ལམ་ཞུགས་རྣམས་ཀྱི་དེད་དཔོན་དང་།

བརྒལ་འདོད་རྣམས་ཀྱི་གྲུ་དང་ནི།

གཟིངས་དང་ཟམ་པ་ཉིད་དུ་གྱུར།།   ༡༧

3.18

སྐྱིད་དོན་གཉེར་ལ་སྐྱིད་དང་ནི།།

མར་མེ་འདོད་ལ་མར་མེ་དང་།

གནས་མལ་འདོད་ལ་གནས་མལ་དང་།

བདག་ནི་ལུས་ཅན་བྲན་འདོད་པ།།   ༡༨

. . . . .

3.25

དེང་དུས་བདག་ཚེ་འབྲས་བུ་ཡོད།།

མི་ཡི་སྐྱིད་པ་ལེགས་པར་ཐོབ།།

དེ་རིང་སངས་རྒྱས་རིགས་སུ་སྐྱེས།།

སངས་རྒྱས་སྲས་སུ་ད་གྱུར་ཏོ།།   ༢༥

BE GENEROUS

3.17

May I protect those who are unsafe;
May I guide those who wander;
And may I be a vessel or a bridge
For those who wish to cross.

3.18

May I be the safe harbor for refugees,
The lamp for those in darkness,
The bed for the weary
And the servant of the needy.

. . . . .

3.25

At last my life will bear fruit!
Now my life is worth living!
I am reborn into the company
Of the awakened beings!

3.27

བོང་བས་ཕྱུག་དང་ཕྱུང་པོ་ལས།།

ཇི་ལྟར་རིན་ཆེན་རྟེན་པ་ལྟར།།

དེ་བཞིན་ཇི་ཞིག་ལྟར་སྟེས་ནས།།

བྱང་ཆུབ་སེམས་འདི་བདག་ལ་སྐྱེས།། ༢༧

3.29

འགྲོ་བའི་ནད་རབ་ཞི་བྱེད་པའི།།

སྨན་གྱི་མཆོག་ཀྱང་འདི་ཡིན་ནོ།།

སྲིད་ལམ་འཁྱམས་ཞིང་དུབ་པ་ཡི།།

འགྲོ་བའི་ངལ་བསོའི་ལྗོན་ཤིང་ཡིན།། ༢༩

3.30

འགྲོ་བ་ཐམས་ཅད་ངན་འགྲོ་ལས།།

སྒྲོལ་བར་བྱེད་པའི་སྤྱི་སྟེགས་ཡིན།།

འགྲོའི་ཉོན་མོངས་གདུང་སེལ་བའི།།

སེམས་ཀྱི་ཟླ་བ་ཤར་བ་ཡིན།། ༣༠

. . . . .

38

3.27
Like a blind man
Who has stumbled on a jewel in a midden,
I have somehow developed
The resolve to awaken for others!

3.29
That resolve is the best medicine
To cure the ills of the world.
It is the tree whose limbs provide shade
For those exhausted on life's road.

3.30
It is everyone's bridge to freedom
From the suffering of life.
It is the waxing moon
That eases the pain of the world.

. . . . .

7.25

ཚོད་མ་ལ་སོགས་སྨྱིན་པ་ལ་འདང་།།

འདྲེན་པས་ཐོག་མར་སྐྱོར་བར་མཛད།།

དེ་ལ་གོམས་ནས་ཕྱི་ནས་ནི།།

རིམ་གྱིས་རང་གི་ཤ་ཡང་གཏོང་།། ༢༥

BE GENEROUS

7.25

As a first step in generosity,

Try giving something from your garden.

With practice, you will find that

You can give even your own flesh.

4. BE THOUGHTFUL!

The term *mindfulness*, drawn from Buddhist discussions of meditation and of ethics, has entered popular culture in a host of contexts. But it is not always clear that people who use this English term have in mind anything like what Buddhist philosophers were discussing when they used the Pali, Sanskrit, or Tibetan terms often translated into English as *mindfulness*. And many who use that term these days do not think of it as *ethically* important, as opposed to being a kind of neutral cognitive skill. So, I prefer not to use that term, for fear that it has been hijacked and transmuted beyond recognition.

Shantideva in fact uses two terms for slightly different attitudes in the chapter of *How to Lead an Awakened Life* that is often called the mind-fulness chapter. The first is the Sanskrit *smrti*, which really means "to remember" or "to recall to mind." I translate this term as "recollection." And what we are urged to recollect are things such as our vows, or commitments, what is most important to us, those who have helped us, and the like. These help to set our moral motivation and to help us avoid being distracted by objects of desire or aversion.

The second term is the Sanskrit *samprajana*, which means "introspective vigilance." It denotes the ability to check on our current state of mind. To be vigilant is to be deliberate about the focus of our attention and to be observant of our emotional states and motivations. This vigilance allows us to determine whether these things in fact line up with our values, commitments, knowledge, and all the other stuff that we recollect and to correct our mental attitude if necessary.

When we put these two skills together, we lead a life that is intentional, thoughtful, and deliberate. We can avoid being buffeted by random occurrences in our environment, by passing emotional states, or by attitudes that we know to be wrong, but which nonetheless seem to take over—that is, we can live with greater wisdom and integrity.

In these verses, Shantideva calls our attention to two important principles to keep in mind: First, our own mind can be either our most powerful enemy or our most powerful tool, depending on our degree of recollection and vigilance. Without these important moral skills, the mind runs amok and leads to all kinds of inappropriate thought, speech, and behavior. But when properly restrained by recollection and vigilance, the mind becomes the source of everything good in our lives. These apparently purely cognitive skills therefore are extremely important to our ethical lives.

Second, our mind is the thing over which we have the most control. We can't do much about either what happens in the world outside us or what others say and do. But we can gain control over our reactions to those occurrences. As a consequence, whether we suffer or not, and whether we are happy or not, is often much more in our own hands than we may think. But so also is our capacity to help others: If we act thoughtlessly, no matter what is going on around us, we are useless; if we act thoughtfully, then no matter what is going on around us, we can be helpful.

Perhaps most dramatically, Shantideva recommends that sometimes vigilance should lead us not to act but to pause. When we are not certain that we are seeing things correctly, or that our emotional state is appropriate, it is better, he urges, to "stay still like a block of wood," to step back, to recollect our values, to focus our attention, and to act only when we know what is right.

༥.༡

བསྐལ་པ་བསྔུང་བར་འདོད་པ་ཡིས།།
རབ་ཏུ་བསྒྲིམས་ནས་སེམས་བསྒྲུང་སྟེ།།
སེམས་འདི་བསྒྲུང་བར་མ་བྱས་ན།།
བསྐལ་པ་བསྒྲུང་བར་ཡོང་མི་ནུས།། $\qquad$ ༡

༥.༢

སེམས་ཀྱི་གླང་པོ་ཡན་བཏང་བས།།
མནར་མེད་གནོད་པ་བྱེད་པ་ལྟར།།
གླང་ཆེན་མ་ཐུལ་མྱོས་པ་ཡིས།།
འདི་ན་དེ་འདྲའི་གནོད་མི་བྱེད།། $\qquad$ ༢

༥.༣

ཀུན་ནས་དྲན་པའི་ཐག་པ་ཡིས།།
སེམས་ཀྱི་གླང་པོ་དམ་བཏགས་ན།།
འཇིགས་པ་ཐམས་ཅད་མེད་འགྱུར་ཞིང་།།
དགེ་བ་ཐམས་ཅད་ལག་ཏུ་འོང་།། $\qquad$ ༣

BE THOUGHTFUL

5.1

If you want to take care of your practice,
You have to take care of your mind.
If you don't take care of your mind
There is no way you can take care of your practice.

5.2

The elephant mind
Causes so much harm and degradation!
Wild, mad elephants
Do not cause so much harm.

5.3

Nonetheless, if the elephant mind
Is restrained by the rope of recollection,
Then all fear is banished,
And every virtue falls into our hands.

4.4

སྐྱག་དང་སེང་གེ་སྦྲང་ཆེན་དེག།
སྦྲུལ་དང་དགྲ་རྣམས་ཐམས་ཅད་དང་།
སེམས་ཅན་དམྱལ་བའི་སྲུང་མ་དང་།
བྱད་མ་དེ་བཞིན་སྲིན་པོ་རྣམས།།

4.5

སེམས་འདི་གཅིག་པུ་བཏགས་པ་ནས།
དེ་དག་ཐམས་ཅད་བཏགས་པར་འགྱུར།
སེམས་འདི་གཅིག་པུ་བཏུལ་བ་ན།
དེ་དག་ཐམས་ཅད་ཐུལ་བར་འགྱུར།།

4.6

འདི་ལྟར་འཇིགས་པ་ཐམས་ཅད་དང་།
སྡུག་བསྔལ་དཔག་ཏུ་མེད་པ་ཡང་།
སེམས་ལས་བྱུང་བ་ཡིན་ནོ་ཞེས།
ཡང་དག་གསུང་བ་ཉིད་ཀྱིས་བསྟན།།

. . . . .

BE THOUGHTFUL

5.4

Tigers, lions, elephants,

Bears, snakes,

And all of your enemies, including

Devils and evil spirits:

5.5

You can tame all of these

Just by taming your own mind.

By gaining control over your own mind,

You gain control of all of these.

5.6

It is true to say

That all of our fear, and even

Our most unimaginable suffering

Arises from the mind alone.

. . . . .

5.11

ནུ་ལ་སོགས་པ་གང་ཞིག་ཏུ།།
དེ་དག་གསོད་མི་འགྱུར་བར་བསྐྱེད།།
སྟོང་བའི་སེམས་ནི་སྟོབ་པ་ལས།།
ཆུལ་ཁྲིམས་ཕ་རོལ་ཕྱིན་པར་བཤད།།

11

5.12

སེམས་ཅན་མི་སྲུན་ནམ་མཁའ་བཞིན།།
དེ་དག་གཞོམ་གྱིས་ཡོང་མི་ལང་།།
ཁྲོ་བའི་སེམས་འདི་གཅིག་བཅོམ་ན།།
དགྲ་དེ་ཐམས་ཅད་ཆོམས་དང་འདྲ།།

12

5.13

ས་སྟེང་འདི་དག་ཀོས་གཡོག་ཏུ།།
དེ་སྙེད་ཀོ་བས་ག་ལ་ལང་།།
ལྷམ་མཐིལ་ཙམ་གྱི་ཀོ་བས་ནི།།
ས་སྟེང་ཐམས་ཅད་གཡོགས་དང་འདྲ།།

13

BE THOUGHTFUL

5.11

Where could you take fish or other poor animals
So that I cannot kill them?
I can only perfect my conduct if I
First give up even thinking of wrongdoing.

5.12

Malicious people are as boundless as the sky;
I can never defeat them all!
But to defeat the angry mind
Is to defeat all of my enemies!

5.13

Where is there enough leather
To cover the entire world?
Just the leather of my sandals
Is sufficient to cover it all!

5.14

དེ་བཞིན་ཕྱི་རོལ་དོངས་པོ་ཡང་།།
བདག་གིས་ཕྱིར་བརྟོག་མི་ལང་གི།།
བདག་གི་སེམས་འདི་ཕྱིར་བརྟོག་བྱའི།།
གཞན་རྣམས་བརྟོག་གོ་ཅི་ཞིག་དགོས།།

༡༩

5.22

བདག་གི་རྟེད་དང་བཀུར་སྟི་དང་།།
ལུས་དང་འཚོ་བ་མེད་ན་བླ་ཞིང་།།
དགེ་བ་གཞན་ཡང་ཉམས་བླ་ཡི།།
སེམས་ནི་ནམ་ཡང་ཉམས་མི་བྱ།།

༢༢

. . . . .

5.24

ནད་ཀྱིས་དཀྲུགས་པའི་མི་དག་ནི།།
ལས་རྣམས་ཀུན་ལ་མཐུ་མེད་པ།།
དེ་བཞིན་རྨོངས་པས་སེམས་དཀྲུགས་པ།།
ལས་རྣམས་ཀུན་ལ་མཐུ་མེད་དོ།།

༢༩

BE THOUGHTFUL

5.14
Just so, I can't control
What goes on outside;
But if I can control my own mind,
What need is there to control anything else?

5.22
That's why I can give up my possessions, my
 reputation,
My body, and my livelihood.
I can even give up on virtue.
But I must never give up on my mind.
. . . . .

5.24
Just as a sick man
Can't accomplish anything,
If you forget your commitments and lose your
 vigilance,
You can't accomplish anything.

5.25

ཤེས་བཞིན་མེད་པའི་སེམས་ལྡན་པའི།།
ཐོས་དང་བསམས་དང་སྒོམས་པ་ཡང་།།
གློ་རྡོལ་བུམ་པའི་ཆུ་བཞིན་དུ།།
དྲན་པ་ལ་ནི་དེ་མི་གནས།།   ༢༥

5.26

ཐོས་ལྡན་དད་པ་ཅན་དང་ནི།།
བརྩོན་པ་ལྷུར་ལེན་དུ་མ་ཡང་།།
ཤེས་བཞིན་མེད་པའི་སྐྱོན་ཆགས་པས།།
ལྟུང་བའི་རྙོག་དང་བཅས་པར་འགྱུར།།   ༢༦

5.27

ཤེས་བཞིན་མེད་པའི་ཆོམ་རྐུན་དག།
དྲན་པ་ཉམས་པའི་རྗེས་འབྲང་བས།།
བསོད་ནམས་དག་ནི་ཉེར་བསགས་ཀྱང་།།
རྐུན་པོས་ཕྲོགས་བཞིན་ངན་འགྲོར་འགྲོ།།   ༢༧

BE THOUGHTFUL

5.25
Like a broken pot
That can't hold water,
A distracted mind
Can't hold what it's heard, considered, and
    understood.

5.26
Even those with wisdom, faith,
And great ethical motivation
Can be ruined by vice if they
Lose their introspective vigilance.

5.27
Even the virtuous
Find themselves miserable
When they are robbed by the thief of distraction
Who preys on those who forget their
    commitments.

5.28

ཉོན་མོངས་ཚོམ་རྒྱུན་ཚོགས་འདི་ནི།།
བྲགས་སྐབས་ཚོལ་བར་བྱེད་པ་སྟེ།།
བྲགས་ཏེ་གྱུར་ནས་དགེ་འཕྲོག་ཅིང་།།
བདེ་འགྲོའི་སྒོག་ཀུན་འཛོམས་པར་བྱེད།།

༢༨

5.29

དེ་བས་དབན་པ་ཡིད་སྨྲོ་ནས།།
ཀུད་དུ་ནམ་ཡང་མི་གཏོང་ངོ་།།
སོང་ནའང་དན་འགྲོའི་གནོད་པ་དག།།
དབན་པར་བྱུས་ཏེ་ཉེ་བར་བཞག།

༢༩

. . . . .

5.41

ཅི་ནས་ཏིང་འཛིན་བརྩོན་པ་ནི།།
སྐད་ཅིག་གཅིག་ཀྱང་མི་འཚོར་བར།།
བདག་གི་ཡིད་འདི་གར་སྤྱོར་ཞེས།།
དེ་ལྟར་ཡིད་ལ་སོ་སོར་བརྟག།

༤༡

5.28

The host of pathologies, like a gang of bandits,
Seeks a way into our minds.
When it finds that entrance,
It steals any chance of a happy life.

5.29

Therefore, you should never shift
Recollection from the gateway of the mind.
And if it strays, remember how bad life can get,
And bring it right back.

. . . . .

5.41

You should examine your mind by asking,
"To what am I attending?"
That way you will never lose focus,
Even for a moment.

5.47

གང་ཚེ་བསྐྱེད་པར་འདོད་གྱུར་ཏམ།།
སྐྱ་བར་འདོད་པར་གྱུར་ན་ཡང་།།
དང་པོར་རང་གི་སེམས་བརྟགས་ནས།།
བརྟན་པས་རིགས་པ་ལྡན་པར་བྱ།།

༤༧

5.48

གང་ཚེ་རང་ཡིད་ཆགས་པ་དང་།།
ཁྲོ་བར་འདོད་པ་དེ་ཡི་ཚེ།།
ལས་སུ་མི་བྱ་སྨྲ་མི་བྱ།།
ཤིང་བཞིན་དུ་ནི་གནས་པར་བྱ།།

༤༨

5.49

རྒོད་དང་ག་ཞར་བཅས་པ་འམ།།
གལ་ཏེ་ང་རྒྱལ་རྒྱགས་ལྡན་པའམ།།
མཚང་འབྲུ་བ་ཡི་བསམ་པ་དང་།།
གལ་ཏེ་སྐྱོར་འབྱིན་བསླུ་སེམས་སམ།།

༤༩

60

BE THOUGHTFUL

5.47
Whenever you are about to speak,
Whenever you are about to act,
First, check your state of mind,
Only then can you act reasonably.

5.48
If you find your mind to be
Filled with desire or aversion,
Neither speak nor act,
But stay still like a block of wood.

5.49
If your mind is agitated,
Or if you are feeling
Contemptuous,
Proud, or deceptive, . . .

5.50

གང་ཚེ་བདག་བསྟོད་སྨྱུང་ལེན་པ་འམ།།
གཞན་ལ་སྨོད་པ་ཉིད་དང་ངེ།།
གཤེ་བཙས་འགྱེད་དང་བཙས་གྱུར་པ།།
དེ་ཚེ་མྱིད་བཞིན་གནས་པར་བྱ།།

40

5.51

རྗེད་དང་བཀུར་སྟི་སྒྲགས་འདོད་པ་འམ།།
གཡོག་འཁོར་དོན་དུ་གཤེར་འདོད་པ་འམ།།
བདག་སེམས་རིམ་གྲོ་འདོད་གྱུར་ན།།
དེ་ཚེ་མྱིད་བཞིན་གནས་པར་བྱ།།

41

5.52

གཞན་དོན་ཡལ་བར་འདོར་བ་དང་།།
རང་དོན་གཉེར་བར་འདོར་པ་དང་།།
སྐྲ་བར་འདོད་པའི་སེམས་བྱུང་ན།།
དེ་ཚེ་མྱིད་བཞིན་གནས་པར་བྱ།།

42

BE THOUGHTFUL

5.50

If you are about to brag,
Or to run others down,
If you are about to be abusive or mean,
Stay still like a block of wood!

5.51

If you are after wealth, honor, or fame,
Or if you are after followers or subordinates,
As long as you are thinking this way,
Stay still like a block of wood!

5.52

When you are about to work against others,
Or to work only for yourself,
Or when you are about to talk just to be heard,
Stay still like a block of wood!

5.53

མི་བརྟོད་ལེ་ལོ་འཇིགས་པ་དང་།།
དེ་བཞིན་སྐྱི་བཏོལ་མུ་ཅོར་དང་།།
རང་གི་ཕྱོགས་ཞེན་སེམས་བྱུང་ན།།
དེ་ཚེ་ཉིད་བཞིན་གནས་པར་བྱ།།   ༥༣

5.54

དེ་ལྟར་ཀུན་ནས་ཉོན་མོངས་དང་།།
དོན་མེད་བརྩོན་པའི་ཡིད་བཏགས་ནས།།
དེ་ཚེ་དཔའ་བོས་གཉེན་པོ་ཡིས།།
དེ་ནི་བཏན་པོར་གཟུང་བར་བྱ།།   ༥༤

5.55

ཤིན་ཏུ་ངེས་དང་རབ་དད་དང་།།
བརྟན་དང་གུས་དང་ཞེ་སར་བཅས།།
ངོ་ཚ་ཤེས་དང་འཇིགས་བཅས་དང་།།
ཞི་ཞིང་གཞན་དགའ་བྱེད་ལ་བརྩོན།།   ༥༥

. . . . .

64

BE THOUGHTFUL

5.53

When you are feeling impatient or lazy,
Frightened, disrespectful, or insensitive,
Or when you are thinking only of yourself,
Stay still like a block of wood!

5.54

When you see things this way,
When you can see how your pathology
Only leads to pointless activity,
Become a moral hero and cure yourself!

5.55

Be resolute and confident;
Be respectful and polite;
Be modest, gentle, and calm.
And commit to others' happiness.

. . . . .

5.56

ཕན་ཚུན་མི་མཐུན་བྱིས་པ་ཡི།།
འདོད་པ་རྣམས་ཀྱིས་མི་སྐྱོ་ཞིང་།།
ཉོན་མོངས་སྐྱེས་པས་འདི་དག་གི།
སེམས་འདི་བྱུང་སྐྱམ་བཅེར་ལྷུན་དང་།།

5.57

ཁ་ན་མ་ཐོ་མེད་དངོས་ལ།།
བདག་དང་སེམས་ཅན་དབང་བྱུས་ཤིང་།།
སྦྱལ་པ་བཞིན་དུ་ང་མེད་པར།།
ཡིད་འདི་ཇག་ཏུ་གཟུང་བར་བྱ།།

5.58

རིང་ཞིག་ལོན་ནས་དལ་བའི་མཚོག།
ཐོབ་པ་ཡང་དང་ཡང་བསམས་ནས།།
སེམས་དེ་ལྟ་བུར་རི་རབ་ལྟར།།
རབ་ཏུ་མི་གཡོ་གཟུང་བར་བྱ།།

BE THOUGHTFUL

5.56

I shouldn't worry about others' conflicting desires.

Instead, I should feel sorry for them,

Since I know that they are like this

Only because of their own pathologies.

5.57

So, maintaining a good reputation,

For my own sake and for that of all other beings,

I will always see my lack of self,

And will know that I exist only as an illusion.

5.58

Always remembering that

It has taken a long time to achieve

This chance to lead a good life,

I will remain as unshakable as a mountain!

5. BE POLITE!

We don't often think of etiquette as a moral matter. But Shantideva, like everyone else in this tradition, sees proper conduct as morally important. There are at least four reasons for this. First, behaving boorishly annoys people, and that causes unhappiness. Nobody likes being around a slob or someone who is rude or disruptive. So, one way to spread a little happiness is just to be polite and to make life easier on those around us.

Second, behaving politely makes social interactions smoother and more productive. Proper conduct is the oil that lubricates our social life; improper conduct is the grit that makes everything more difficult. And when our social life goes well, everything goes well.

Third, working to become polite involves self-restraint. It encourages us to become aware both of what we are tempted to do or say and of what we really ought to do or say and, thus, sometimes of a gulf between those two. By striving to be more polite we therefore also gain self-understanding and self-control.

Finally—and very importantly—observing the rules of propriety makes it more likely that others will listen to you, or allow you to assist them, and so makes you a more effective moral agent. For one thing, people simply prefer to be around others whose behavior is appropriate. So, whether you are a teacher, a carpenter, or a doctor, people are more likely to learn from you, to hire you, or to consult you and heed your advice if your behavior is respectful and appropriate. But beyond that, for you to be effective, people need to respect and to trust you. Failure to observe social norms or standards of professional conduct lowers you in the estimation of others and so, once again, makes it hard for you to be an effective agent.

What constitutes proper conduct varies across cultures and often depends on your social role. Good etiquette in one country may be rude in another (for example, shaking hands vs. bowing; eating with chopsticks vs. with one's hands). And what is appropriate behavior for a doctor ("Please remove your clothes") may be inappropriate for a minister. So, vigilance in these matters is also a moral concern—even if we are well-meaning, if we don't attend to the circumstances of our actions, we could make things worse instead of better. Some of Shantideva's examples are perfectly general, but others may strike as quaint; they are intended for medieval Indian monks, and we should read them as examples with that in mind.

5.35

དོན་མེད་གཡེང་བར་ལྟ་བ་ནི།།
ནམ་ཡང་བདག་གིས་མི་བྱ་སྟེ།།
དེས་པར་སེམས་པས་རྟག་ཏུ་ནི།།
མིག་ནི་ཕབ་སྟེ་བལྟ་བར་བྱ།།

३५

5.36

ལྟ་བ་ངལ་བསོའི་ཆེད་དུ་ནི།།
རེས་འགའན་ཕྱོགས་སུ་བལྟ་བར་བྱ།།
འགའ་ཞིག་མིག་ལམ་སྣང་གྱུར་ན།།
བལྟས་ནས་འོངས་པ་ལེགས་ཞེས་བརྗོད།།

३७

5.39

ལུས་ཀྱིས་འདི་ལྟར་གནས་བྱ་ཞེས།།
བྱ་བ་བརྩོགས་ནས་དེ་ནས་ནི།།
སྐབས་སུ་ལུས་འདི་ཇི་ལྟ་བུར།།
གནས་པ་ཡིན་ཞེས་བལྟ་བར་བྱ།།

३८

. . . . .

BE POLITE

5.35
Don't stare at this and that!
If there is nothing to look at,
Keep your eyes down,
As you do in meditation.

5.36
But give your eyes a break sometimes
And look around.
And if you catch so much as a glimpse of someone,
Be sure to give them a nice greeting!

5.39
Every so often, move around.
Think about your body.
Pay attention to your posture,
And think about how others see you.

. . . . .

5.42

འཛིགས་དང་དགའ་སྟོན་སོགས་འཐེལ་བར།།
གལ་ཏེ་མི་ཉུས་ཅི་བདེར་བྱ།།
འདི་ལྟར་སྙིན་པའི་ཉེས་དག་ཏུ།།
ཚུལ་ཁྲིམས་བཏང་སྙོམས་བཞག་པར་གསུངས།།

౭౨

5.70

འགྲོ་དང་འོང་བའི་རྟེན་ཚམ་དུ།།
ལུས་ལ་གྲུ་ཡི་བློ་བཞག་སྟེ།།
སེམས་ཅན་རྣམས་དོན་སྒྲུབ་པའི་ཕྱིར།།
ཡིད་བཞིན་གྱི་ནི་ལུས་སུ་བསྒྱུར།།

౭౦

5.71

དེ་ལྟར་རང་དབང་ཡོད་གྱིས་ཏེ།།
རྟག་ཏུ་འཛུམ་པའི་བཞིན་དུ་གྱིས།།
ཁྲོ་གཉེར་དོ་རྣམ་ཡོངས་ཐོང་སྟེ།།
འགྲོ་བའི་བཤེས་དང་གསོང་པོར་གྱིས།།

౭౧

BE POLITE

5.42

In case of danger or on a festive occasion,
You can't pay so much attention to these matters.
So, in those cases, just relax.
Sometimes, etiquette can be put aside.

5.70

Since it helps you come and go,
Think of your body like a ship.
Your mind should set the body in motion
For the benefit of sentient beings.

5.71

Having achieved some self-control
Always make sure you have a smile on your face!
Get rid of frowns and sneers.
And be an honest friend to all.

5.72

ཁྲི་ལ་སོགས་པ་བབ་ཚལ་དུ།།
སྐྱ་དང་བཙས་པར་མི་དོར་རོ།།
སྐྱོ་ཡང་དྲག་ཏུ་མི་དབྱེ་སྟེ།།
ཐག་ཏུ་གཅོམ་སྐྱུང་དགའ་བར་བྱ།།

༧༢

5.73

རུ་སྐྱར་ཁྱི་ལ་ཆོམ་རྐུན་དག།།
སྐྱ་མེད་འཛིན་ཅིང་འགྲོ་བ་ཡིས།།
མཛོན་པར་འདོད་པའི་དོན་སྒྲུབ་པ།།
ཐུབ་པས་ཐག་ཏུ་དེ་བཞིན་སྤྱད།།

༧༣

5.74

གཞན་ལ་གཞེན་བསྐུལ་འདེབས་མཁས་ཤིང་།།
མ་བཚལ་ཐན་པར་བྱེད་པའི་ངག།།
གུས་པས་ཁྱི་བོར་བླང་ཁྱིས་ཏེ།།
ཐག་ཏུ་ཀུན་ཁྱི་སློབ་མར་གྱུར།།

༧༤

76

BE POLITE

5.72

Don't make a racket
And throw furniture around!
Don't slam the door,
And take pleasure in quiet.

5.73

A crane, a cat, and a thief
Achieve their goals
By moving silently.
That's how a wise person acts.

5.74

When helpful experts offer it to you,
Accept good advice with respect.
Be a good student
To anyone who can teach you.

CHAPTER 5

5.75

ལེགས་པར་སྨྲས་པ་ཐམས་ཅད་ལ།།
དགེ་བར་གསུངས་ཞེས་བརྗོད་པར་བྱ།།
བསོད་ནམས་བྱེད་པ་མཐོང་གྱུར་ན།།
བསྟོད་པས་ལེགས་པར་དགའ་བ་བསྐྱེད།། ༧༥

5.76

ལྐོག་ན་ཡོན་ཏན་བརྗོད་བྱ་ཞིང་།།
ཡོན་ཏན་བརྗོད་ན་རྗེས་སུ་བརྗོད།།
རང་གི་ཡོན་ཏན་བརྗོད་ན་དེ།།
ཡོན་ཏན་ཤེས་པར་རིག་པར་བྱ།། ༧༦

5.79

སྨྲ་ན་ཡིད་ཕེབས་འབྲེལ་བ་དང་།།
དོན་གསལ་ཡིད་དུ་འོང་བ་དང་།།
ཆགས་དང་ཞེ་སྡང་སྤངས་པ་དང་།།
འཇམ་ཞིང་རན་པར་སྨྲ་བར་བྱ།། ༧༩

. . . . .

BE POLITE

5.75

Always thank those
Who utter kind words.
When you see someone do something nice,
Encourage them with kind words of your own!

5.76

Praise others even when they are not around,
And when you hear such talk, pass it on.
When others speak of your achievements,
Just accept it as the reward for your goodness.

5.79

When it is time to speak, do so kindly, cogently,
Carefully, in a pleasant voice.
Speak softly and calmly,
Without attachment or anger.

. . . . .

5.91

སོ་ཕྱིང་དང་ནི་མཆིལ་མ་དག།

དོར་བ་ནི་དགབ་པར་བྱ།།

གཅི་ལ་སོགས་པ་འབང་ལོངས་སྤྱོད་པའི།།

ཆུ་དང་ཐང་ལ་དོར་བ་སྤང་།། (༢༡)

5.92

ཁ་བཀང་བ་དང་སྒྲ་བཅས་དང་།།

ཁ་གདངས་ནས་ནི་བཟའ་མི་བྱ།།

རྐང་པ་བརྐྱང་སྟེ་མི་འདུག་ཅིང་།།

ལག་པ་མཉམ་པར་མི་མནྱེ་འོ།། (༢༢)

5.93

བཞོན་པ་མལ་སྟན་གནས་དག་ཏུ།།

བུད་མེད་གཞན་དང་གཅིག་མི་བྱ།།

འཇིག་རྟེན་མ་དད་གྱུར་པ་ཀུན།།

མཐོང་དང་དྲིས་ཏེ་སྤང་བར་བྱ།། (༢༣)

BE POLITE

5.91
If you have to toss your toothpick or spit,
At least cover it up!
And peeing on water or land
That people use is really disgusting!

5.92
Don't eat with your mouth full,
And don't eat with your mouth open or chomp
    your food!
Don't point your legs at others,
And don't rub your hands together or fold
    your arms!

5.93
Don't travel or spend time alone
With someone else's partner,
Or do anything else that causes people
To lose faith in you.

5.94

སོར་མོས་བརྟ་ནི་མི་བྱ་སྟེ།།

གུས་དང་བཅས་པས་གཡས་པ་ཡི།།

ལག་པ་དག་ནི་ཀུན་གྱིས་ཀྱང་།།

ལམ་ཡང་དེ་ལྟར་བསྟན་པར་བྱ།།

ཞེ

BE POLITE

5.94
Don't point at things with your finger!
Show respect by using
Your whole right hand
To show what you are talking about.

6. BE PATIENT!

The patience chapter of *How to Lead an Awakened Life* is almost everyone's favorite; the poetry is exceptionally beautiful, and Shantideva's evocation of sensitive care in our attitudes toward others is immediately compelling. But it is also one of the most challenging chapters: Shantideva confronts the ethical assumption common in many cultures that anger is at least sometimes justified, and sometimes even mandatory.

Many people think that if someone harms either them or someone close to them, or if they witness an injustice, it is reasonable to become angry and to act out of anger. Some go further and argue that the failure to become angry in circumstances such as these shows a lack of self-respect when one is the subject of harm or a lack of real concern for others when they are the subjects of the harm.

Shantideva rejects this view entirely. He argues that anger is never a good thing and indeed that it is a psychopathology: It causes us harm; it leads us to cause others harm; it impairs our judgment and effectiveness; it destroys social relationships. This is not to say that we should accept harms or injustice, only that anger should not mediate our response. Instead, harm and injustice calls for dispassionate diagnosis and rational remediation; for an attitude of care for all concerned, not for hostility; for nonegocentric disapproval, not for a self-centered reflexive reaction.

Anger, Shantideva argues, is always *harmful*. It doesn't feel good; it makes others uncomfortable; it leads to actions we later regret. We don't want to be angry; we aren't at our best when we are angry. When anger subsides, we don't feel proud of the fact that we lost our temper; we feel ashamed. And when we become angry with those with whom we have close personal or professional relationships, we destroy those relationships. We drive those away who could be our friends, our teachers, or our students.

Moreover, Shantideva tells us, anger is always *irrational*. Anger presupposes a way of understanding agency that makes no sense when we think it through carefully. It requires us to think of people as completely independent actors in complete control of their own psychology and behavior—that is, we are angry at someone when we think that they themselves are the cause of the action that inspires our wrath. But this is a misleading way to think about action. Everything we do is caused by previous events, attitudes, and experiences. And we may not understand all of those.

The man who cuts me off in traffic may be racing to the hospital to be with his injured child; the woman who spoke rudely to me may just have been told that she has been laid off from the job that supports her family; my inconsiderate colleague may be the victim of abuse. So, Shantideva admonishes us, just as we would never be angry with the stick with which someone beats us, we should not be angry with an action impelled by causes that we do not understand. To see all of human behavior as the result of complex conditions is to see that anger is never really justified.

Finally, Shantideva tells us, the tendency to become angry is *remediable.* It may be hard to eliminate anger, but it is not impossible. By

CHAPTER 6

reflecting on the irrationality of anger, by reflecting on the harm that it does to us, and by
focusing on the interdependence of people and
the interdependence of actions, motives, and
emotions, we can become more patient.

Therefore, if anger is always harmful, always
irrational, and if we are capable of undoing the
tendency to anger by cultivating patience, we
ought to do so. As he puts it, we are already
kind and patient to those who are suicidally de-
pressed, and we try to help them not to harm
themselves. We can come to see that those who
harm us also harm themselves through their
anger, and so we should extend the same care
to them that we freely extend to those who are
more obviously mentally ill.

Patience, Shantideva concludes, brings us happiness and brings happiness to those around us.
Being patient reflects a saner way to understand

others, and it makes our lives more meaningful. It allows us to cease being reactive and to get some control over our emotions and our lives, enabling us to become genuinely responsive. By being patient—by remaining cool instead of becoming angry, we do not ignore harms; we become better agents for their remediation. So, some may think that when things get bad, or when people do bad things, the only way to show that we care is to become angry. Shantideva disagrees: He thinks that the only way to care for others is to respond to a bad situation or to bad behavior with patience.

CHAPTER 6

6.1

བསྐལ་བ་སྟོང་དུ་བསགས་པ་ཡི།།

སྦྱིན་དང་བདེ་གཤེགས་མཆོད་ལ་སོགས།།

ལེགས་སྤྱད་གང་ཡིན་དེ་ཀུན་ཀྱང་།།

ཁོང་ཁྲོ་གཅིག་གིས་འཇོམས་པར་བྱེད།། ༡

6.2

ཞེ་སྡང་ལྟ་བུའི་སྡིག་པ་མེད།།

བཟོད་པ་ལྟ་བུའི་དཀའ་ཐུབ་མེད།།

དེ་བས་བཟོད་ལ་ནན་ཏན་དུ།།

སྣ་ཚོགས་ཚུལ་གྱིས་བསྒོམ་པར་བྱ།། ༢

6.3

ཞེ་སྡང་ཟུག་རྔུའི་སེམས་འཆང་ན།།

ཡིད་ནི་ཞི་བ་ཉམས་མི་མྱོང་།།

དགའ་དང་བདེ་བའང་མི་འཐོབ་ལ།།

གཉིད་མི་འོང་ཞིང་བརྟན་མེད་འགྱུར།། ༣

6.1

One moment of anger can destroy
Everything you have accomplished
Through the good work, generosity, and piety
You practiced for your entire life.

6.2

No vice is worse than aversion, and
No virtue is better than patience.
Hence you should assiduously
Cultivate patience any way you can.

6.3

When the thorn of aversion sticks in the heart,
Your mind finds no peace,
Nor can it achieve happiness or joy.
Sleep does not come, and one's strength ebbs away.

6.4

གང་དག་ནོར་དང་བཀུར་སྟི་ཡིས།།

དྲིན་བྱིན་དེ་ལ་བརྟེན་གྱུར་པ།།

དེ་དག་ཀྱང་ནི་སྲང་ལྷན་པའི།།

རྗེ་དཔོན་དེ་ལ་གསོད་པར་རྩོལ།། ༩

6.5

དེ་ཡིས་མཛའ་བཤེས་སྐྱོ་བར་འགྱུར།།

སྐྱིན་པས་བསྐུས་ཀྱང་བརྟེན་མི་བྱེད།།

མདོར་ན་ཁྲོ་བས་བདེར་གནས་པ།།

དེ་ནི་འགའ་ཡང་ཡོད་མ་ཡིན།། ༥

. . . . .

6.10

གལ་ཏེ་བཅོས་སུ་ཡོད་ན་ནི།།

དེ་ལ་མི་དགར་ཅི་ཞིག་ཡོད།།

གལ་ཏེ་བཅོས་སུ་མེད་ན་ནི།།

དེ་ལ་མི་དགའ་བྱས་ཅི་ཕན།། ༡༠

6.4

Even those you make rich
And those who you have honored
Will turn on you
If you are warped by anger.

6.5

An angry man loses his friends;
Even if he has been generous, nobody will
    help him.
In short, nothing
Can make an angry man happy.

6.10

If you can fix a situation,
What's the point of frustration?
If you can't fix it,
What's the point of frustration?

6.14

གོམས་ན་སླ་བར་མི་འགྱུར་བའི།།

དངོས་དེ་གང་ཡང་ཡོད་མ་ཡིན།།

དེ་བས་གཟོད་པ་ཆུང་གོམས་པས།།

གཟོད་པ་ཆེན་པོ་བཟོད་པར་བྱོས།།

༡༤

6.15

སྦྲུལ་དང་ཤ་སྦྲང་དག་དང་ནི།།

བཀྲེས་སྐོམ་ལ་སོགས་ཚོར་བ་དང་།།

གཡན་པ་ལ་སོགས་བཅས་པ་ཡི།།

དོན་མེད་སྡུག་བསྔལ་ཅིས་མ་མཐོང་།།

༡༥

6.16

ཚ་གྲང་ཆར་དང་རླུང་སོགས་དང་།།

ནད་དང་འཆིང་དང་རྡེག་སོགས་ལ།།

བདག་གིས་བཟེ་རེ་མི་བྱ་སྟེ།།

དེ་ལྟར་བྱས་ན་གཟོད་པ་འཕེལ།།

༡༦

BE PATIENT

6.14
Everything becomes easier
Once you get used to it.
So, when you get used to a little pain,
Even a terrible pain will become bearable.

6.15
Isn't it obvious that the pain caused by
The bites of insects or snakes,
Or by hunger, thirst, or a rash,
Is pretty insignificant?

6.16
So, I'm not going to be bothered by
Things such as heat, cold, rain, or wind.
Nor by things such as pain or illness.
If I am, they only feel worse.

6.17

ལ་ལ་བདག་གི་ཁྲག་མཐོང་ན།།

དཔའ་བརྟན་ལྷག་པར་སྐྱེ་འགྱུར་ཡོད།།

ལ་ལ་གཞན་གྱི་ཁྲག་མཐོང་ན།།

བོག་ཅིང་བརྒྱལ་བར་འགྱུར་བ་ཡོད།། ༡༤

6.18

དེ་ནི་སེམས་ཀྱི་དང་བརྟན་དང་།།

སྟུར་མའི་ཆུལ་ལས་གྱུར་པ་ཡིན།།

དེ་བས་གནོད་པ་ཁྱད་བསད་ཅིང་།།

ལྷག་བསྒལ་རྣམས་ཀྱིས་མི་ཆུགས་བྱོས།། ༡༥

6.19

མཁས་པས་སྡུག་བསྒལ་བྱུང་ཡང་ནི།།

སེམས་ཀྱི་རབ་དང་རྙོག་མི་བྱ།།

ཉོན་མོངས་རྣམས་དང་གཡུལ་འགྱེད་ལ།།

གཡུལ་འགྱེད་ཚེ་ན་གནོད་པ་མང་།། ༡༦

6.17

Some are brave even when they
See their own blood flowing;
Others faint even when they
See others' blood.

6.18

This is the difference between
Strength and cowardice.
So, we should steel ourselves
Against suffering and never give in to pain.

6.19

If one is wise, one's peace of mind
Is not disturbed by suffering.
The real battle is the fight with the pathologies;
That's where the hard work is done.

6.20

སྦག་བསྐལ་ཐམས་ཅད་ཁྱུད་བསད་ནས།།
ཞེ་སྡང་ལ་སོགས་དག་འཆོམས་པ།།
དེ་དག་རྒྱལ་ཉེད་དཔའ་བོ་སྟེ།།
སྦག་མ་རོ་ལ་གསོད་པ་འོ།།

20

6.22

མཁྲིས་པ་ལ་སོགས་སྦག་བསྐལ་གྱི།།
འབྱུང་གནས་ཆེ་ལ་མི་ཁྲོ་བར།།
སེམས་ཡོད་རྣམས་ལ་ཅི་སྟེ་ཁྲོ།།
དེ་དག་ཀུན་ཀྱང་རྐྱེན་གྱིས་བསྐུལ།།

22

6.23

དཔེར་ན་མི་འདོད་བཞིན་དུ་ཡང་།།
ནད་འདི་འབྱུང་བར་འགྱུར་བ་ལྟར།།
དེ་བཞིན་མི་འདོད་བཞིན་དུ་ཡང་།།
ནན་གྱིས་ཉོན་མོངས་འབྱུང་བར་འགྱུར།།

23

6.20

The real heroes ignore their own suffering.
They thus defeat the enemy of enmity.
All of the others
Only kill corpses.

6.22

Things like bile cause a lot of suffering,
But I don't get angry at them!
So why get angry at those with minds?
They are also entirely driven by conditions!

6.23

Consider this: Even though we don't want it,
Illness just comes over us.
Just so, even though we don't want them,
Our pathologies just come over us.

6.24

ཁྲོ་བར་བྱ་ཞེས་མ་བསམས་ཀྱང་།།
སྐྱེ་བོ་རྣམས་ནི་ཀྱི་ནར་ཁྲོ།།
བསྐྱེད་པར་བྱ་ཞེས་མ་བསམས་ཀྱང་།།
ཁྲོ་བ་དེ་བཞིན་སྐྱེ་བར་འགྱུར།། ༢༩

6.25

ཉེས་པ་ཇི་སྙེད་ཐམས་ཅད་དང་།།
སྡིག་པ་རྣམ་པ་སྣ་ཚོགས་པ།།
དེ་ཀུན་རྐྱེན་གྱི་སྟོབས་ལས་བྱུང་།།
རང་དབང་ཡོད་པ་མ་ཡིན་ནོ།། ༢༥

6.33

དེ་བས་དགྲ་འགམ་མཛའ་ཡང་རུང་།།
མི་རིགས་བྱེད་པ་མཐོང་གྱུར་ན།།
འདི་འདྲའི་རྐྱེན་ལས་གྱུར་ཏོ་ཞེས།།
དེ་ལྟར་སོམས་ཏེ་བདེ་བར་མནོས།། ༣༣

BE PATIENT

6.24

Nobody ever says to themselves, "I want to get
    angry,"
But anger still arises.
Nor does anger say, "Now I want to arise,"
But it still arises.

6.25

Every kind of misdeed and vice
Comes about because of conditions.
Not a single one
Arises independently.

6.33

Therefore, whether you see an enemy or a friend
Do something senseless,
Reflect that it was caused by conditions,
And having done so, stay calm.

6.34

གལ་ཏེ་རང་དགས་འགྱུབ་འགྱུར་ན།།

འགའ་ཡང་ལྷག་བསྙལ་མི་འདོད་པས།།

ལུས་ཅན་དག་ནི་ཐམས་ཅད་ཀྱང་།།

སྐུ་ལའང་ལྷག་བསྙལ་འབྱུང་མི་འགྱུར།།   ༣༩

6.35

བག་མེད་པས་ནི་བདག་འཕང་བདག།

ཚོར་མ་ལ་སོགས་གནོན་པ་སྟེ།།

བྱད་མེད་ལ་སོགས་སྟོབ་བྱའི་ཕྱིར།།

ཧྲམ་ཞིང་རམས་གཙོད་ལ་སོགས་སྟེ།།   ༣༥

6.36

ཁ་ཅིག་འགགག་ཅིང་གཡང་སར་མཆོང་།།

དུག་དང་མི་འཕྲོད་ཟ་བ་དང་།།

བསོད་ནམས་མ་ཡིན་སྤྱོད་པ་ཡིས།།

རང་ལ་གནོད་པ་བྱེད་པ་ཡོད།།   ༣༧

6.34

If everybody got what they wanted,
Nobody would suffer.
After all, nobody
Wants to suffer.

6.35

Nonetheless, people are careless. In anger,
They impale themselves on life's thorns.
They overdo the food and drink,
Or they chase women they can't have.

6.36

Some kill themselves by hanging, by leaping
    from cliffs,
Or by taking poison or drugs.
Others harm themselves by
Engaging in vicious conduct.

6.37

གང་ཚེ་ཉོན་མོངས་དབང་གྱུར་པས།།
བདག་སྲུག་ཉིད་ཀྱང་གསོད་བྱེད་པ།།
དེ་ཚེ་དེ་དག་གཞན་ལུས་ལ།།
གནོད་མི་བྱེད་པར་ཇི་ལྟར་འགྱུར།།

༣༧

6.38

ཉོན་མོངས་སྐྱེས་པས་དེ་ལྟ་བུར།།
བདག་གསོད་ལ་སོགས་ཞུགས་པ་ལ།།
སྙིང་རྗེ་བསྐྱེད་ལ་མ་སྐྱེས་ན།།
ཁྲོ་བར་འགྱུར་བ་ཅིའི་ཐ་ཚིག།

༣༨

6.39

གལ་ཏེ་གཞན་ལ་འཚེ་བྱེད་པ།།
བྱིས་པ་རྣམས་ཀྱི་རང་བཞིན་ན།།
དེ་ལ་ཁྲོ་བར་མི་རིགས་ཏེ།།
སྲེག་པའི་རང་བཞིན་མེ་བཀོན་འདྲ།།

༣༩

BE PATIENT

6.37

Since their pathology can drive them
To hurt even their beloved selves,
How can you expect them
Not to harm others?

6.38

So, even if you can't bring yourself to care
For those whose pathologies
Drive them to take their own lives,
Why be angry with them?

6.39

Since it is natural for a fool
To harm others,
Anger toward them is as senseless
As anger toward fire, which naturally burns.

6.40

ཟོན་ཏེ་སྐྱོན་འདི་བློ་བུར་ལ།།
སེམས་ཅན་རང་བཞིན་དེས་པ་ནའང་།།
ཟོ་ནའང་ཁྲོ་བར་མི་རིགས་ཏེ།།
མཁའ་ལ་དུད་འཁྱིལ་བཀོན་པ་བཞིན།།

༧༠

6.41

དབྱུག་པ་ལ་སོགས་དངོས་བཀོལ་ཏེ།།
གལ་ཏེ་འཕེན་པ་ལ་ཁྲོ་ན།།
དེ་ཡང་ཞེ་སྡང་གིས་སྣད་པས།།
ཞེས་ན་ཞེ་སྡང་ལ་ཁྲོ་རིགས།།

༧༡

. . . . .

6.56

བདག་ནི་དེང་ཉིད་ཀྱི་ཡང་སྲིད་བི།།
ལོག་འཚོས་ཡུན་རིང་གསོན་མི་རུང་།།
བདག་ལྟ་ཡུན་རིང་གནས་གྱུར་ཀྱང་།།
འཆི་བའི་སྲུག་བསྲལ་དེ་ཉིད་ཡིན།།

༥༧

BE PATIENT

6.40

If the problem is adventitious
And sentient beings are naturally good,
Then anger toward them is as senseless
As anger at a smoky sky.

6.41

Since I ignore the stick that hits me,
And am angry at he who wields it,
It would make more sense for me to be angry
At the anger that drives him than at him.

. . . . .

6.56

It would be better to die today
Than to live a long misguided life.
For even if I live a long time,
The suffering of death awaits me.

6.57

 སྐྱེ་ལམ་ལོ་བཅུ་ར་བདེ་སྨྱོང་ནས།།

སད་པར་གྱུར་པ་གང་ཡིན་དང་།།

གཞན་ཞིག་ཡུད་ཙམ་བདེ་སྨྱོང་ནས།།

སད་པར་གྱུར་པ་གང་ཡིན་པ།། ༥༧

6.58

སད་པ་དེ་དག་གཉིས་ཀ་ལའང་།།

བདེ་བ་དེ་ནི་ཕྱིར་འོང་མེད།།

ཚེ་རིང་ཚེ་ཐུང་གཉིས་ཀ་ཡང་།།

འཆི་བའི་དུས་ན་དེ་འདྲར་ཟད།། ༥༨

6.59

རྙེད་པ་མང་པོ་ཐོབ་གྱུར་ཏེ།།

ཡུན་རིང་དུས་སུ་བདེ་སྤྱད་ཀྱང་།།

ཆོམ་པོས་ཕྲོགས་པ་ཇི་བཞིན་དུ།།

སྟོན་མེ་ལག་པ་སྟོང་པར་འགྲོ།། ༥༩

BE PATIENT

6.57
While one person wakes up
After a century of pleasant dreams,
Another wakes up after
Only a moment of happiness.

6.58
But happiness does not return to either of them
Once they awaken.
At the moment of death, it no longer matters
Whether one has lived a long or a short life.

6.59
Even if I have amassed many possessions
And have enjoyed a long life of pleasure,
I will leave this life empty-handed and naked,
Like the victim of a robbery.

CHAPTER 6

6.61

གང་གི་དོན་དུ་བདག་གསོན་པ།།
དེ་ཉིད་གལ་ཏེ་ཉམས་གྱུར་ན།།
སྲོག་པ་འབའ་ཞིག་བྱེད་པ་ཡི།།
གསོན་པ་དེས་ཀོ་ཅི་ཞིག་བྱ།།

༧༠

110

BE PATIENT

6.61

So, since all that I live for
Vanishes in the end,
What is the point
Of living a life of vice?

7. BE COMMITTED!

To become a really good, really caring person is hard. It can't be one more project among others: Take out the trash, catch up with the email, paint the back room, become really good, and then practice the piano. No. To become the truly caring person that Shantideva wants you to become requires that you devote yourself wholeheartedly to this project as the most important organizing goal of your life; you must subordinate everything else to this objective.

That is what commitment means. And this is why Shantideva describes commitment as the wind in our sails. It is what organizes everything else we do. He reminds us once again that we don't have all the time in the world and that the time to act is now. He also reminds us that we need to live our lives with confidence but not with pride. Pride is an irrational inflation of our own importance under the illusion that our achievements are ours alone, that we are autonomous. Confidence is the certainty that by acting with others, and through the confluence of their assistance and our efforts, we can achieve our goals. Pride is egocentric; confidence reflects our sense of our social nature.

Commitment arises from the union of an awareness of the urgency of life, from our aspiration to make our lives meaningful, and from the confidence that we can do so; and all of these arise from an understanding of ourselves as existing in relation to others and of the fact that one's life is meaningful only when it benefits others.

CHAPTER 7

7.1

དེ་ལྟར་བཟོད་པས་བཅོན་འགྱུས་བཅས།།
འདི་ལྟར་བཅོན་ལ་བྱུང་ཆུང་གནས།།
ཆུང་མེད་གཡོ་བ་མེད་པ་བཞིན།།
བསོད་ནམས་བཅོན་འགྱུས་མེད་མི་འབྱུང་།། ༡

7.2

བཅོན་གང་དགེ་ལ་སྒོ་བ་ལོ།།
དེ་ཡི་མི་མཐུན་ཕྱོགས་བཤད་བྱ།།
ལེ་ལོ་ངན་ལ་ཞེན་པ་དང་།།
སྐྱིད་ལུག་བདག་ཉིད་བརྙས་པ་ལོ།། ༢

. . . . .

7.4

ཉིན་མོངས་རྒྱ་བས་བཐོར་ནས་ནི།།
སྐྱེ་བའི་རྒྱར་ནི་ཆུད་གྱུར་ནས།།
འཆི་བདག་ཁར་ནི་སོང་གྱུར་པ།།
ཅི་སྟེ་ད་དུང་མི་ཤེས་སམ།། ༩

114

BE COMMITTED

7.1

A patient person should develop commitment.
After all, awakening requires commitment.
Just as a boat can't move without wind,
You can't do anything worthwhile without
    commitment.

7.2

Commitment is enthusiasm for virtue.
What is its opposite?
Laziness, attraction to base things,
Apathy, and self-loathing.

. . . . .

7.4

The pathologies that hunt you have caught your
    scent!
You are caught in a net of misery!
Can't you tell that you are already
In the jaws of death?

7.5

རང་སྟེ་རིམ་གྱིས་གསོད་པ་ཡང་།།

ཁྱོད་ཀྱིས་མཐོང་བར་མ་གྱུར་ཏམ།།

ཉོན་ཀྱང་གཉིད་ལ་བརྟེན་པ་གང་།།

གདོལ་པ་དང་ནི་མ་ཉེ་བཞིན།།　　　　　५

7.6

ལམ་ནི་ཀུན་ནས་བཀག་ནས་སུ།།

འཇི་བདག་གིས་ནི་བསླུས་བཞིན་དུ།།

ཇི་ལྟར་ཁྱོད་ནི་ཟ་དགའ་ཞིང་།།

འདི་ལྟར་གཉིད་ལོག་ཇི་ལྟར་དགའ།།　　　　　७

7.7

གྱུར་བ་གཉིད་དུ་འཇི་འགྱུར་བས།།

ཇི་སྲིད་དུ་ནི་ཚོགས་བསག་བྱ།།

དེ་ཚེ་ལེ་ལོ་སྤངས་ཀྱང་ནི།།

དུས་མ་ཡིན་པར་ཅི་ཞིག་བྱ།།　　　　　७

BE COMMITTED

7.5

Can't you see that your own herd
Is being slaughtered one by one?
And here you are—a buffalo
Dozing in a slaughterhouse!

7.6

When your path is blocked on all sides,
And the Lord of Death has fixed you in his gaze,
How can you eat and drink?
How can you make love?

7.7

Death will come swiftly
With sharpened knives!
Lead a good life until then,
For what can you do when that time comes?

7.8

འདི་ནི་མ་བྱུས་བརྩམས་པ་དང་།།

འདི་ཕྱིད་བྱུས་པར་གནས་པ་ལ།།

བློ་བུར་འཆི་བདག་ཚོངས་ནས་ནི།།

ཀྱི་ཧུད་བཙོམ་ཞེས་སེམས་པར་འགྱུར།། ༨

. . . . .

7.14

མི་ཡི་གྲུ་ལ་བརྟེན་ནས་སུ།།

སྡུག་བསྔལ་རྒྱ་པོ་ཆེ་ལས་སྒྲོལ།།

གྲུ་འདི་ཕྱི་ནས་རྙེད་དཀའ་བས།།

རྨོངས་པ་དུས་སུ་གཉིད་མ་ལོག།། ༡༤

. . . . .

7.53

ཞུམ་བཅས་ཚོལ་བ་དོར་བ་ལ།།

ཕོངས་ལས་ཐར་པ་ཡོད་དམ་ཅི།།

ང་རྒྱལ་ཚོལ་བ་བསྐྱེད་པས་ནི།།

ཆེན་པོ་ཡིས་ཀྱང་ཐུབ་པས་དཀའ།། ༥༣

118

BE COMMITTED

7.8

When death arrives without warning,
You may think, "Wait, I haven't done this;
This job I started is only half done;
Oh, how terrible this is!"

. . . . .

7.14

Having found the vessel of a human life,
Use it to cross the great river of suffering!
This craft is hard to catch again,
So there is no time to lose!

. . . . .

7.53

When your strength is sapped by depression,
You are beset by many problems.
But if you are self-confident and committed,
You can surmount the greatest difficulties.

7.56

འགྲོ་གང་ང་རྒྱལ་གྱིས་བཅོམ་དེ།།

ཉིད་མཆོངས་ང་རྒྱལ་ཅན་མ་ཡིན།།

ང་རྒྱལ་ཅན་དགྲའི་དབང་མི་འགྲོ།།

དེ་དག་ང་རྒྱལ་དགྲ་དབང་འགྱུར།།

༥༧

7.59

གང་ཞིག་ང་རྒྱལ་དགྲ་ལས་རྒྱལ་ཕྱིར་ང་རྒྱལ་འཆང་།།

དེ་ནི་ང་རྒྱལ་ཅན་དང་རྣམ་རྒྱལ་དཔའ་དེ་ཉིད།།

གང་ཞིག་ང་རྒྱལ་དགྲ་བདོ་བ་ཡང་དེས་བཅོམ་སྟེ།།

འགྲོ་ལ་འདོད་བཞིན་རྒྱལ་བའི་འབྲས་བུ་རྫོགས་པར་བྱེད།།

༥༩

120

BE COMMITTED

7.56.
To be overcome by pride
is not to be self-confident; it is pathological!
A self-confident person is not defeated by
their enemies;
A proud person has been defeated by the
enemy of pride.

7.59
The true heroes are the self-confident
Who use their confidence to defeat the enemy
of pride.
They can then joyfully share the results
Of that conquest with the entire world.

8. REMEMBER WHO YOU ARE!

These verses are drawn from the chapter on meditation. The Tibetan term for meditation, *gom*, literally means "to familiarize." To meditate is to allow ideas or ways of thinking that one knows are right to become so habitual and ingrained that they come to constitute the way we see the world. So far, we have seen how important it is to be aware of our impermanence and interdependence with others. And we have seen that appreciating this interdependence leads to and facilitates generosity, attention, propriety, patience, and commitment.

Now it is time to reflect very seriously on that interdependence and to transform our experience of our" own existence. We may naively and reflexively think of ourselves as independent individuals who just happen to interact with other independent individuals. But we can see past this illusion: We can come to see ourselves as integral parts of larger wholes. In doing so, positive attitudes toward others that might have once appeared to be nice options come to be seen as mandatory.

Shantideva urges us to see that we are related to one another as the parts of the body are related to one another; as parts of a single whole—the community of sentient beings—it makes as little sense to care only about our own individual welfare and to ignore that of others as it would for our hand not to be willing to pull a thorn from our foot. We are urged to see that what is bad about suffering can't be that it is *ours,* but that it is suffering, and that to recognize that fact is immediately to have a reason for alleviating it, regardless of whose it is.

Shantideva concludes by reminding us that if we can find happiness in the well-being of others, we will have a much better shot at a happy life than if we can only find happiness in our own well-being. By transforming our self-understanding in these ways, we internalize all the lessons taught in the earlier parts of the text, and we thereby come not only to *know* what it is to be caring but also to *be* caring.

8.9

བྱིས་དང་སྐལ་བ་མཉམ་སྤྱོད་ན།།
དེས་པར་དན་འགྲོར་འགྲོ་འགྱུར་ཏེ།།
སྐལ་མི་མཉམ་པར་ཁྱེད་བྱེད་ན།།
བྱིས་པ་བསྟེན་པས་ཅི་ཞིག་བྱ།།

8.10

སྐད་ཅིག་གཅིག་གིས་མཛའ་འགྱུར་ལ།།
ཡུད་ཙམ་གྱིས་ནི་དགྲར་ཡང་འགྱུར།།
དགའ་བའི་གནས་ལ་ཁྲོ་བྱེད་པས།།
སོ་སོའི་སྐྱེ་བོ་མགུ་བར་དཀའ།།

8.11

ཕན་པར་སྨྲས་ན་ཁྲོ་བར་བྱེད།།
བདག་ཀྱང་ཕན་ལས་བློག་པར་བྱེད།།
དེ་དག་དག་ནི་མ་མཉན་ན།།
ཁྲོ་བས་ངན་འགྲོར་འགྲོ་བར་འགྱུར།།

8.9

If you act like a fool,
You will lead a base and miserable life.
If you are after something different,
Why hang out with fools?

8.10

At one moment a fool is your friend;
At the next they are your enemy!
You try to please them and they get angry.
Such people are impossible to please.

8.11

If you give them good advice, they get angry.
And then they just reject it.
But if you don't listen to them,
They become angry and miserable.

8.12

མཐོ་ལ་ཕྱག་དོག་མཉམ་དང་འབྲན།།

དམན་ལ་ང་རྒྱལ་བསྟེན་ན་དེགས།།

མི་སྙན་བརྗོད་ན་ཁོང་ཁྲོ་སྐྱེ།།

ནམ་ཞིག་བྱིས་ལས་ཐེན་པ་འཕྲོ།། ༡༢

. . . . .

8.90

བདག་དང་གཞན་དུ་མཉམ་པ་ནི།།

དང་པོ་ཉིད་དུ་འབད་དེ་བསྒོམ།།

བདེ་དང་སྡུག་བསྔལ་མཉམ་པས་ན།།

ཐམས་ཅད་བདག་བཞིན་བསྲུང་བར་བྱ།། ༩༠

8.91

ལག་པ་ལ་སོགས་དབྱེ་བ་རྣམ་མང་ཡང་།།

ཡོངས་སུ་བསྲུང་བྱའི་ལུས་སུ་གཅིག་པ་ལྟར།།

དེ་བཞིན་འགྲོ་བ་ཐ་དད་བདེ་སྡུག་དག།

ཐམས་ཅད་བདག་བཞིན་བདེ་བ་འདོད་མཉམ་གཅིག། ༩༡

128

8.12

They envy their betters; they vie with their peers;
They lord it over their subordinates.
When praised, they become arrogant;
How can fools be of any use?

. . . . .

8.90

One should earnestly meditate:
"Self and others are the same;
Since they experience the same happiness and
    suffering,
I should protect everyone as I do myself."

8.91

Even though it has many parts, like hands,
The body protects itself as a single whole.
All of the various beings—with all their happiness
    and suffering—
Are just like a single person who desires happiness.

8.92

གལ་ཏེ་བདག་གི་སྡུག་བསྔལ་གྱིས།།
གཞན་གྱི་ལུས་ལ་མི་གནོད་པ།།
དེ་ལྟ་འང་དེ་བདག་སྡུག་བསྔལ་དེ།།
བདག་ཏུ་ཞེན་པས་མི་བཟོད་ཉིད།། ༩༢

8.93

དེ་བཞིན་གཞན་གྱི་སྡུག་བསྔལ་དག།
བདག་ལ་འབབ་པར་མི་འགྱུར་ཡང་།།
དེ་ལྟ་འང་དེ་བདག་སྡུག་བསྔལ་དེ།།
བདག་ཏུ་ཞེན་པས་བཟོད་པར་དཀའ།། ༩༣

8.94

བདག་གིས་གཞན་གྱི་སྡུག་བསྔལ་བསལ།།
སྡུག་བསྔལ་ཡིན་ཕྱིར་བདག་སྡུག་བཞིན།།
བདག་གིས་གཞན་ལ་ཕན་པར་བྱ།།
སེམས་ཅན་ཡིན་ཕྱིར་བདག་ལུས་བཞིན།། ༩༤

8.92
Even if my own suffering
Does no harm to anyone else,
It is still my own suffering.
And being mine, it is unbearable.

8.93
Just so, even though I don't feel
The sufferings of others,
It is still their own suffering.
And since it is theirs, it is unbearable to them.

8.94
I must eliminate the suffering of others
Just because it is suffering, like my own.
I should work to benefit others
Just because they are sentient beings, as am I.

8.95

གང་ཚེ་བདག་དང་གཞན་གཉིས་ཀ །
བདེ་བ་འདོད་དུ་མཚུངས་པ་ལ། །
བདག་དང་ཁྱད་པར་ཅི་ཡོད་ན། །
གང་ཕྱིར་བདག་གཅིག་བདེ་བར་བརྩོན། །

པུ

8.96

གང་ཚེ་བདག་དང་གཞན་གཉིས་ཀ །
སྡུག་བསྔལ་མི་འདོད་མཚུངས་པ་ལ། །
བདག་དང་ཁྱད་པར་ཅི་ཡོད་ན། །
གང་ཕྱིར་གཞན་མིན་བདག་སྲུང་བྱེད། །

པུ༡

8.97

གལ་ཏེ་དེ་ལ་སྡུག་བསྔལ་བས། །
བདག་ལ་མི་གནོད་ཕྱིར་མི་བསྲུང་། །
མ་འོངས་པ་ཡི་སྡུག་བསྔལ་ཡང་། །
གནོད་མི་བྱེད་ན་ད་ཅིས་བསྲུང་། །

པ༡

132

8.95
Since I am just like others
In desiring happiness,
What is so special about me
That I strive for my happiness alone?

8.96
Since I am just like others
In not desiring suffering,
What is so special about me
That I protect myself but not others?

8.97
If, because their suffering does not harm me,
I do not protect them,
When future suffering does not harm me,
Why do I protect against it?

8.98

བདག་གིས་དེ་ནི་མྱོང་སྣམ་པའི།།
རྣམ་པར་རྟོག་དེ་ལོག་པ་སྟེ།།
འདི་ལྟར་མི་བདང་གཉེན་ཉིད་ལ།།
སྐྱེ་བ་ཡང་ནི་གཉེན་ཉིད་ཡིན།།

8.99

གང་ཚེ་གང་གི་སྟུག་བསྲལ་གང་།།
དེ་ནི་དེ་ཉིད་ཀྱིས་བསྲུང་ན།།
རྐང་པའི་སྟུག་བསྲལ་ལག་པས་མིན།།
ཅི་ཕྱིར་དེས་ནི་དེ་བསྲུང་བྱ།།

8.100

གལ་ཏེ་རིགས་པ་མིན་ཡང་འདིར།།
བདག་ཏུ་འཛིན་པས་འཇུག་ཅེ་ན།།
བདག་གཞན་མི་རིགས་གང་ཡིན་དེ།།
ཅི་ནུས་པར་ནི་སྤང་བྱ་ཉིད།།

8.98
The idea that this very self
Will experience that future suffering is false:
Just as when one has died, another
Who is then born is really another.

8.99
If another should only protect himself
Against his own suffering,
When a pain in the foot is not in the hand,
Why should one protect the other?

8.100
You may say that even though it makes no sense,
We act this way because of self-grasping.
But it only makes sense to abandon
An attitude that makes no sense for anyone!

8.101

རྒྱུད་དང་ཚོགས་ཞེས་བྱ་བ་ནི།།
ཕྲེང་བ་དམག་ལ་སོགས་བཞིན་བརྟན།།
སྡུག་བསྔལ་ཅན་གང་དེ་མེད་པ།།
དེས་འདི་སུ་ཞིག་དབང་བར་འགྱུར།།

101

8.102

སྡུག་བསྔལ་བདག་པོ་མེད་པར་ནི།།
ཐམས་ཅད་བྱེ་བྲག་མེད་པ་ཉིད།།
སྡུག་བསྔལ་ཡིན་ཕྱིར་དེ་བསལ་བྱ།།
དེས་པས་འདིར་ནི་ཅི་ཞིག་བྱ།།

102

8.103

ཅི་ཕྱིར་ཀུན་གྱི་སྡུག་བསྔལ་ནི།།
བཟློག་པར་བྱ་ཞེས་བརྩད་དུ་མེད།།
གལ་ཏེ་བཟློག་ན་འང་ཐམས་ཅད་བཟློག།
དེ་མིན་བདག་ཀྱང་སེམས་ཅན་བཞིན།།

103

. . . . .

8.101

The so-called continuum and collection of
    psychophysical clusters,
Are ultimately unreal, just like a forest or an army.
Since the sufferer does not exist,
By whose power does suffering come about?

8.102

As no suffering self exists,
We should not distinguish among people.
Just because there is suffering, it is to be eliminated.
What is the point of discriminating here?

8.103

"Why should everyone's suffering be alleviated?"
There is no dispute!
If any of it is to be alleviated, all of it is to be
    alleviated!
After all, I also am a sentient being!

. . . . .

8.125

གལ་ཏེ་བྱིན་ན་ཅི་སྦྱིན་ཅེས།།
བདག་དོན་སེམས་པ་འདི་ཡི་ཚུལ།།
གལ་ཏེ་སྤྱད་ན་ཅི་སྤྱིན་ཞེས།།
གཞན་དོན་སེམས་པ་ལྷ་ཡི་ཆོས།། ༡༢༥

8.127

བདག་ཉིད་མཐོ་བར་འདོད་པ་ནེས།།
ངན་འགྲོ་ངན་དང་སྐྱེན་པར་འགྱུར།།
དེ་ཉིད་གཞན་ལ་སྤོ་བྱས་ན།།
བདེ་འགྲོར་རིམ་གྲོ་འཐོབ་པར་འགྱུར།། ༡༢༧

8.128

བདག་གི་དོན་དུ་གཞན་བཀོལ་ན།།
བྲན་ལ་སོགས་པ་མྱོང་བར་འགྱུར།།
གཞན་གྱི་དོན་དུ་བདག་སྤྱད་ན།།
རྗེ་དཔོན་ཉིད་སོགས་མྱོང་བར་འགྱུར།། ༡༢༨

8.125

"If I give this away, what will I have left to enjoy?"
To think only of oneself is to be like a demon!
"Since I enjoy this, what can I give away?"
To think of others is to be divine!

8.127

By seeking high status,
I become low, stupid, and miserable.
By seeking that for another,
I become elevated, respected, and wise.

8.128

By ordering another to serve my purposes,
I end up as a servant.
By serving another's purposes,
I end up as a master.

8.129

འཇིག་རྟེན་བདེ་བ་རྗེ་སྐྱེད་པ།།
དེ་ཀུང་གཞན་བདེ་འདོད་ལས་བྱུང་།།
འཇིག་རྟེན་སྡུག་བསྔལ་རྗེ་སྐྱེད་པ།།
དེ་ཀུན་རང་བདེ་འདོད་ལས་བྱུང་།།

༡༢༠

8.129

All of the happiness in the world
Comes from wanting others' happiness.
All of the suffering in the world
Comes from wanting one's own happiness.

9. AND SEAL IT WITH A PROMISE!

We end with a verse that the present Dalai Lama has always said is his favorite in the text. While in the context of a religious tradition committed to rebirth, this verse connotes a commitment to be reborn for all time in order to act endlessly for the benefit of sentient beings, we can give this verse a more secular reading as well. Our existence as agents is not exhausted by the boundaries of our human life, either spatially or temporally. Our actions ripple endlessly throughout space and time, like waves on the ocean. What we do here affects those in far off countries and those who will inherit this world from us. When we take political action, it can have global consequences. When we act to slow climate change,

we act for the benefit of those who are yet un-
born. This verse asks us to consider our actions
in that context and to act in ways that are, and
will continue to be, of benefit to all.

10.55

ཇི་སྲིད་ནམ་མཁའ་གནས་པ་དང་།།
འགྲོ་བ་ཇི་སྲིད་གནས་གྱུར་པ།།
དེ་སྲིད་བདག་ནི་གནས་གྱུར་ནས།།
འགྲོ་བའི་སྡུག་བསྔལ་སེལ་བར་ཤོག།

10.55
As long as space endures,
And for as long as there are living beings,
May I also remain in the world
To dispel their suffering.

NOTE ON THE TRANSLATION

The translation is from the Tibetan edition by Śāntideva and rGyal tshab rje, *Byang chub sems pa'i spyod
pa la 'jug pa'i rnam bshad rgyal sras 'jug ngogs*, published by the Gelugpa Student Welfare Committee,
Sarnath, in 1999.

I present a literary translation in which I have tried
to capture the meaning and the style of the Tibetan
text but not to be lexically or grammatically precise.
For those who wish to read the entire text, and who
wish to read it in a more philologically precise translation, there are four excellent English translations
from which to choose.

The first is by Stephen Batchelor, *Guide to the
Bodhisattva's Way of Life*, published by the Library
of Tibetan Works and Archives in 1999. It is a reliable
and clear translation of the Tibetan text but has little
by way of scholarly apparatus. A second option is the

translation by Kate Crosby and Andrew Skilton, *The Bodhicharyavatara*, published by Oxford University Press in 2008. This edition translates the Sanskrit text, and the English stays very close to the Sanskrit. This edition also has an extended introduction and very useful notes. The Padmakara Translation Group has produced a very poetic translation from the Tibetan with a good introduction in *The Way of the Bodhisattva*, published by Shambhala in 2007. The group has also published a commentary on the text by the Dalai Lama XIV, *For the Benefit of All Beings: A Commentary on "The Way of the Bodhisattva,"* in 2009. Alan and Vesna Wallace present a very precise and well-annotated translation of this text in their *A Guide to the Bodhisattva's Way of Life*, published by Snow Lion in 1997. This edition also allows the reader to compare the Sanskrit and Tibetan editions.

If you want to read the selections from other Buddhist scriptures that Shantideva collated to accompany his text, Charles Goodman has translated the *Śikṣāmuccaya* in *The Training Anthology of*

Śāntideva, published by Oxford University Press in 2016. Finally, for a collection of informative articles about this text that are very accessible, try Jonathan Gold and Douglas Duckworth (eds.), *Readings of Śāntideva's "Guide to Bodhisattva Practice,"* published by Columbia University Press in 2019.